C000050629

Annals of the STUPID Party

ANNALS OF STUPID PARTY: REPUBLICANS BEFORE TRUMP
Copyright © 2016 by Clyde N. Wilson

ALL RIGHTS RESERVED. No part of this publication may be reproduced, distributed, or transmitted in any form or by any means, including photocopying, recording, or other electronic or mechanical methods, or by any information storage and retrieval system without the prior written permission of the publisher, except in the case of very brief quotations embodied in critical reviews and certain other non-commercial uses permitted by copyright law.

Produced in the Republic of South Carolina by

SHOTWELL PUBLISHING LLC
Post Office Box 2592
Columbia, So. Carolina 29202

www.ShotwellPublishing.com

Cover Design: Hazel's Dream

ISBN-13: 978-0997939330
ISBN-10: 0997939338

10 9 8 7 6 5 4 3 2 1

Annals of the STUPID Party

REPUBLICANS BEFORE TRUMP

Clyde N. Wilson

THE WILSON FILES 3

SHOTWELL

COLUMBIA   SO. CAR.

EST. 2015

PUBLISHING

COMMENTS ON CLYDE WILSON'S WRITING

Clyde Wilson had been ploughing the ground long before many of us came to plant. —Donald Livingston

Clyde Wilson is a national treasure. —Alice Teller

Clyde Wilson shows great ability in the field of intellectual history. —*American Historical Review*

Clyde Wilson exhibits the rarest kind of courage—intellectual courage. —Columbia, SC, *State*

Clyde Wilson is certainly the biggest intellectual heavyweight with the neo-Confederate scene. —Southern Poverty Law Center

. . . a careful scholar who has thought hard and deep about his beloved South. Wilson is, in short, an exemplary historian who displays formidable talent. —Eugene Genovese

. . . a mind as precise and expansive as an encyclopedia . . . These are the same old preoccupations given new life and meaning by a real mind—as opposed to what passes for minds in the current intellectual establishment. —Thomas H. Landess

This generous collection of Clyde Wilson's essays . . . places him on the same level with all the unreconstructed greats in modern Southern letters: Donald Davidson, Andrew Lytle, Frank L. Owsley, Richard Weaver, and M.E. Bradford. —Joseph Scotchie

Clyde Wilson is an obstreperous soldier in the great Jacobin wars that have plagued the nation. —Robert C. Cheeks

Professor Clyde N. Wilson's latest book is remarkable in many ways. At one and the same time it is richly variegated and philosophically sound, while its style and form are consistently elegant. —Jack Kershaw

That man's willing to say in print what most folks are afraid to THINK. —Reader Comment

CONTENTS

FOREWORD

IN THE PRESIDENTIAL ELECTION of 2016, for the first time in a long while, American voters have an actual choice. Donald Trump, a candidate opposed by the media, the banks, and Establishment politicians has won the Republican nomination with unprecedented grassroots support from regular people. Until now, the Republican leadership has not differed from the Democrats on anything important. Both support endless Middle Eastern war, destructive "trade" deals, unlimited immigration including Muslims, punitive affirmative action, Political Correctness, rewarding Wall Street for its egregious sins, and incredibly stupid and reckless bating of Russia.

In the campaign so far Trump has challenged Establishment orthodoxy. Should he be elected, the greatest obstacle to meaningful change will be the Republican Party, for reasons which I have tried to elucidate in this book. Whether he is elected or not, let us hope that his campaign has revealed once and for all the intellectual and moral shallowness of the Republican Establishment and the mass media.

Most of the material herein was originally published by *Chronicles* in its magazine or Blog, and is republished here with generous permission.

Clyde N. Wilson
The Dutch Fork, South Carolina
October 2016

i

I. SOUNDING THE TRUMP

RECENT ANNALS OF THE STUPID PARTY

DONALD TRUMP has certainly revolutionized American politics. And he did so by a very simple act—mentioning substantive truths that other Republicans fear to utter.

Trump is not perfect. But criticism at this point is like Titanic survivors complaining about accommodations on the lifeboats. No ordinary man would climb into the hog pen and tangle with the whole herd of filthy Republican sows at once.

That small but illustrious company who follow my scribblings know that I have long (for a half century) been a gadfly of the Republican Party, a tiny wasp trying to sting through the thick elephant's hide. I have tried to disabuse those people who consider themselves "conservatives" of the obstinately held misconception that the Party is or ever has been of any use to them. (One of the many destructive achievements of the Republicans in American discourse is emptying the term "conservative" of any meaning.) This is a collection of my writings on the subject, which have been made relevant by the Trump insurgency and the reaction to it.

In 2014 I predicted that a maverick would rise in the Republican Party to challenge the Establishment. Trump has justified my prediction. I also discussed the lengths to which the Establishment would go to protect their power. They have no real quarrel with Hillary Clinton. But Trump is a genuine threat to their self-appointed supremacy. In response to Trump they are acting exactly in the way I have been describing them for a long time. I wrote:

"A maverick candidate, who is wise, brave, and somehow able to communicate with the people over massive jamming by the media, could perhaps get a message across about the real dangers to the commonwealth (debt, imperial over-extension, the ongoing proletarianisation of the middle class, to mention just a few). We can be certain that the two parties will never touch a real issue, which might upset their cozy relations with each other and the media. For such an outsider to succeed would require extraordinary circumstances indeed. However, he might accomplish the wrecking of the Republican Elite, which would be a great service to the restoration of good government."

Trump has amazingly fulfilled my prediction. The great question of the day at this writing is: Will the Establishment succeed in killing off the insurgency. We write before the November election, but the question remains whether or not Trump is actually elected. At this writing we await the results of a close election. But for those of us who want to reform the overgrown, fat, arrogant beast in Washington, an election victory will be just a beginning. Can Trump tame Leviathan? What knowledge and weapons does he have for the battle? The Republican Party itself is a poor resource for what needs to be done unless it is itself radically reformed.

Republicans have always preferred vague and "respectable" campaigns that avoid any reference to real issues policies, or opinions. "Tippecanoe and Tyler Too"; "The Rail Splitter;" "Rum, Romanism, and Rebellion"; "Morning in America"; "a thousand points of light"; "No Child Left Behind." Rubio, once the latest Establishment candidate for Leader of the World and Great Decider, told us: "This election is about the future." Thank you, Senator for making your ideas clear.

Even worse, were the series of multi-colored slick-paper mailings from Jeb Bush. One tells us that he has a plan to deal with ISIS. Oh, goody! From such a noble source we don't need to know what the plan is or how it might differ from any of the other plans of Democratic and Republican incumbents and wannabes, nearly all the same.

In another, Jeb Bush, with arms majestically crossed and fearless gaze, assured us: "We are living in serious times that deserve serious leadership." We were expected to rally gratefully to his generous offering of his august person as "serious leader." No substance need be addressed; no evidence is needed except his word. I am your prince. Bow down and honor me. In the past this approach has worked with millions of Republican voters. Can we hope that at last the people of the grassroots have copped to the Establishment's contempt for them, which has been so vividly revealed by the anti-Trump hysteria? Even better, might we hope that the Republican party is going into history's dustbin with the Federalists and Whigs, to be replaced by an actual opposition political party.

Note that the platforms of nearly all the Republican wannabes early in the campaign were of this vague imperious nature. The one exception being foreign affairs, in which they take a militant stance for war in the Mideast and hostility to Russia. Republicans don't have any real principles or any ideas about anything, but for foreign affairs they do have neocon "intellectuals" who have prepared their positions for them. Can these people have given any real thought to the dangerous consequences of the positions they are taking? Have they learned nothing from reality, as opposed to campaign ads that have been supplied them?

The American people are often fooled, but they have a natural, healthy, deep down aversion to making a wimp President. Remember Adlai Stevenson, Nelson Rockefeller, Al Gore. This is why Jeb Bush and Rubio could never make good nominees. Rubio has a shifty, over-sensitive demeanor that bothers normal people. Cruz has an unmistakable aura of meanness. A President must appear to have at least a little bit of gravitas. Sad to say, a great deal of the current American public even attributes some to Obama.

My friend Dr. Boyd Cathey very aptly writes:

"What happens now may, indeed, be the hardest part of the 2016 campaign: attempt to bring together enough rational Republicans and Independents and many disaffected Democrats in a coalition to stop the re-enthronement of the absolute incarnation of globalist, Wall Street, establishmentarianism: Hillary Clinton. And all the while maintaining the reality of what made Donald Trump the candidate he is and has been—the fresh and unbought unapologetic outsider, the anti-PC and anti-establishment candidate par excellence, the candidate who promises to transform not only this country domestically, but also its disastrous Neoconservative foreign policy."

PARDON, SAM, A SLIGHT AMENDMENT (2013)

OUR LAMENTED FRIEND Sam Francis scored big when he labeled the Democrats as "the evil party" and the Republicans as "the stupid party." These telling characterizations have appealed to many later observers, as have other of Sam's apt phrases, like "anarcho-tyranny." Sam was always in earnest but his comments were often laced with humour. He knew what H.L. Mencken or Will Rogers or perhaps both said: Observing American politics is a hoot if you just keep a sane perspective and remember that their main use is entertainment.

There can be little dispute about "the evil party." It might be said, however, that there is a slight Democratic credit here. Democrats sometimes actually believe the depraved stuff they spout and even try to make a rational-sounding argument. They pursue a real agenda and represent real interests. Not so the Republicans.

Are the Republican Elite really as stupid as they seem? Certainly the ideal Republican candidate for office is the same as any hostess wants for the spare man at her dinner party: presentable, not too old, no real work to do, with inherited money and a mediocre I.Q. Now and then, when fortunes are low, the Republicans will play the U.S. Grant card and go for a military hero, but lately that does not work as well as it used to.

The Republicans' apparent stupidity rests on the fact that they invariably and with utter predictability betray their rank and file of Middle Americans and thereby presumably damage themselves. But is this really so stupid when the leaders can calculate with near certainty that the poor slobs will come back again no matter what is done to them? And when they know that if they show any real allegiance to their voters or try to do anything substantive for them, they will be declared by the media to be no longer respectable and thus be constantly on the defensive and guilty of un-American negativity?

A lot becomes clear when we realize that the Republican party is not a political party. Few of its leaders have any idea what a political principle is or what political debate is supposed to be. The few who do have an idea avoid such things like the plague. The Republican party is a marketing strategy. It is a coalition of mostly mediocre people running a campaign for power and perks. Everything these people say is a calculated advertisement without any sincerity or substance. Mentioning your Democratic opponent's bad points is unattractively negative, no matter what terrible things he is accusing you of. Since you have no ideas or principles but only a lust for office, the easiest thing is to go along with the other fellow's agenda and let him win most of the time. And whatever you may have told the slobs to get their votes is yesterday's tired ad campaign that needs to be refreshed.

THE MISSING OPPOSITION

THE LATE AND GREAT Sam Francis famously described the Republicans as the "Stupid Party," pointing out that its leaders were always shooting themselves in the foot or chickening out and defeating their own declared positions. Actually, although in general not terribly bright, Republican leaders are smart enough to take care of their own power and profits, which was all along their only real goal. The mistake is in assuming that they ever had any ideas or principles to begin with. The stupidity is on the part of the Republican voters who have allowed GOP leaders to get away with this forever. In their defense, it can be said that many have stopped voting altogether, and that others vote Republican only because they can't locate "None of the Above" on the ballot.

With the Third World President busy destroying the future of your and my American descendants in favor of foreign invaders, there has never been a greater need in American history for a real opposition party.

But, in fact, there has not been a real opposition party in U.S. politics since Mr. Jefferson sent Colonel Hamilton and His Excellency John Adams heading back north. In the 1830s, when there was a bitter conflict of opinion and interest between a prohibitive tariff and free trade, Andrew Jackson and Martin Van Buren wafted into the White House by declaring themselves stalwart supporters of "a judicious tariff," whatever that might mean. In 1840 the Whigs beat them at their own game. They announced their bold program to fight the depression: "Tippecanoe and Tyler Too!" (I omit the War for Southern Independence, in which massive and unprecedented government force was employed to "solve" the principled opposition of Southern communities and their citizens.)

It is a fact that a firmly equivocal and nice sounding blandness has always been one of the greatest keys to success for American politicians. When was the last presidential election in which any real issues were contested? When the positions of the parties were anything other than variations on the same theme?

Blandness has great appeal because the mass of half-educated pseudo-intellectuals who make up much of the American population are fearful of conflict and scared to death of controversial opinions. We even hear that opponents of some current orthodoxy are merely raising opposition for opposition's sake and threatening the warm feelings of "nonpartisanship" desired by all good citizens. One celebrity historian has promoted the idea that the lack of any real opposition in politics is one of the great virtues of the American regime. This avoidance of ideas and principles has always been the Republican stock in trade.

For a long time, they held the votes of the respectable middle and upper classes because of the vague impression that the Democrats were the disreputable party of Catholics, Jews, and Southerners.

Meanwhile, the leaders continued with the serious business of enriching themselves.

Another fact: With the exception of Reagan's contribution to winning the Cold War, the entire history of the Republican Party in the 20th century has been grotesque betrayal—a lack of effective opposition to any leftist and Democratic initiative. The Republican Party has won office claiming opposition and immediately abetted and institutionalized whatever revolution has been imposed. Whenever the party leadership has been challenged, money, electoral expertise, and cunning deceit have been employed to defeat the usurper. In 1964, when the grass roots rose up, the leaders torpedoed their own candidate. In 1980, when there was a potential threat, the candidate was quickly co-opted. When George Wallace showed the potential of social conservative voters, Republican leaders held their noses and successfully gathered in the harvest, at least for a time, without ever having the least intention of pressing any of the issues. When conservative Christians became politically active, giving great hope to many, they, too, were swiftly invited into the party and neutralized. For some time now the party has rested on the votes of conservative Christians and Southerners. It has never had any intention of giving these voters anything, never has given them anything, and never will give them anything. To do so would not be respectable, would invite heightened calumny from the press, and would interfere with the real objective: power and profits.

The Republican party has a large professional machinery to train candidates in PR. Most candidates are merely examples of standard Republican "statesmanship." What they say has only a tactical relationship to what they do. It never occurs to them to operate any other way. It seldom occurs to them to speak the truth or entertain any idea that is not a calculated slogan. During the next campaign they will stand on "the sacredness of marriage," followed by sell-out as soon as the election is over. Say whatever works to get elected and once elected consider the government as a resource for your own agenda and interests.

WHEN GEORGE W. BUSH launched an unnecessary war of aggression on the basis of lies to the American people and Congress, there was no effective opposition. The Founding Fathers would have instantly recognized this as treason—the most unquestionably impeachable offense ever committed by one holding high office. No effective political opposition—although Bill Clinton could be impeached for a bit of ambiguous verbiage. Then both parties colluded to subsidize the financiers so that their immense wealth would not be threatened by their evil acts against the people. No opposition. There is no reason to think that the illegal immigration juggernaut will be any different. In the future, intelligent observers (if there are any) will judge that the years of George W. Bush marked the *de facto* end of the American experiment in freedom and self-government.

The Republican grass roots have never been in a more ornery mood of disgust with their leadership.

Meanwhile, the Republicans are busy trying to provoke a conflict with Russia. Possibly, this will be a short-term diversion that will boost their support, as is usual in such a situation—at potentially grave cost to Americans and to humanity. Some sincere people have been led into a campaign to impeach

Obama. This is a standard Republican red herring for the rubes to let off steam to no purpose. The number of Republican senators with enough guts to convict the first black president of high crimes can assemble in a couple of old fashioned phone booths, with room to spare.

If by some miracle the party in 2016 nominates a presidential candidate who is an uncompromised opponent of the current regime, it will be interesting to see what ensues. Such a candidate's toughest opposition will be from the leaders of his own party, especially as they will feel it is their turn to have two terms in the executive mansion. He or she will have to be a person of extraordinary courage and principle, with the eloquence to speak directly to the people over the noise of the media. But it is more likely that the dog will return to its vomit, and the Republicans will nominate another photogenic, superficially sincere and intelligent empty suit from the Deep North, possibly with a white Hispanic running mate.

What is likely is that the demographic changes which they abetted will determine that the Republicans will never again win a national election. So, Sam, you were right after all. They are the Stupid Party.

THE WAY WE ARE NOW—REPUBLICANS

THERE HAVE BEEN REPUBLICANS who were conservatives, but the Republican Party is not and never has been a force for conservatism in American life. Except for those who, in Russell Kirk's words, "mistake the acquisitive instinct for a conservative disposition."

From its very beginning the Republican Party was the vehicle of state capitalists. It flourished by persuading a large part of the middle class that it represented their values--patriotism, progress, and Protestant virtues. It long marketed itself as the party against reactionary "Rum, Romanism, and Rebellion," as the party of Progress under decent and safe leaders.

The South, which learned the hard way, for a long time did not fall for this delusion. Being killed and exploited concentrates the mind wonderfully. But as the South has been mainstreamed, as the War and Reconstruction have receded in memory and the Southern churches have been absorbed into the Americanist heresy, more and more Southerners have enlisted in the Army of the Lord to trample out the grapes of wrath.

In the 1960s the Republican con game showed signs of losing its power. It was saved by an influx of despised Southerners and by cynically changing its marketing strategy to pretend to represent the issues raised and made popular by George Wallace. In a sense the South can hardly be blamed. We were literally whipped with scorpions out of the Democratic Party. The

Democratic party is now the party of state capitalists (mostly former Republican types) AGAINST Protestant virtues, the Northern ruling classes having morally disintegrated during the 1960s and 1970s.

The Republican state capitalists, meanwhile, would never have even pretended to be "conservative" if Wallace had not forced them to, but would have continued to present themselves as the competent, decent, safe version of Progress— "Compassionate conservatism." In the current presidential competition (2008), they have almost totally reverted to their-old shtick, which served them well for a long, long time--keeping the state capitalist regime in power by deluding the middle class with an image of progressive competence and respectability. As if Goldwater and Reagan never existed, they are all Rockefeller Republicans now. (After all, ain't that where the money is?)

Every bit of leftist legislation that has passed the U.S. Congress in the last half century has had substantial Republican support. It

was the old Southern Democrats who braked radical legislation, not the Republicans. Now that the Southern Democrats have disappeared, the only obstacle to radical legislation is an extraordinary outpouring of grassroots effort, as in stopping (temporarily) the recent illegal alien amnesty bill. The Republicanisation of the South has been a catastrophic net loss for conservatism.

SOUNDING THE TRUMP

Review: *The Trump Revolution: The Donald's Creative Destruction
Deconstructed* by Ilana Mercer

I
N IMPORTANT WAYS, a revolutionary process has begun. So argues
Ilana Mercer in the best extended analysis yet published of the Trump
phenomenon: "Trump is getting an atrophied political system to oscillate in "an
oddly marvelous uprising." For us revolutionaries there is still a long way to go,
but we are entitled to a "modest hope" that "an utterly different political
animal, Donald Trump, might actually do some good for the countrymen he
genuinely seems to love."

It is not Trump who is transforming American politics, the author asserts,
"it's the people of America doing the transforming." Trump is the first
politician in a long, long time who has regarded America as a country rather
than a "proposition" and has actually spoken to and for "the people." Far from
being "divisive," his plain speaking has enthusiastically united large numbers of
Americans.

The Donald's creative destruction of a vile establishment has worked in a
number of ways. He has weakened the media, he has exposed the intellectual
and ethical nullity of the Republican Establishment, almost alone he has told
the truth about the catastrophic reign of George W. Bush, he has broken the
hold of minority complainers over public discourse, and he has exposed the
tissue of lies that is the prevailing phony "free trade" doctrine. The
Establishment will not give up its power, profits, and perks easily, but it has
been damaged. Not "Morning in America," but an opportunity for reform.
And the last initiative "of America's historic, founding majority."

It has hardly been grasped that the media have assumed a strange and
dominant role in American politics. They have constituted for more than half

a century an impermeable barrier between the voters and the candidates. Nothing has been presented without their prior censorship. Whatever this maybe it is not democracy. Who are these people who proliferate in print, airwaves, and internet and who pass down imperious moral pronouncements without any known credentials to do so? Who ever voted for them? Who gave them such great and irresponsible power? Merely by speaking the truth, by refusing to bow to their pretensions, Trump has weakened their power. That is all it took. Simply speak the truth and the "commentators" and "reporters" are revealed as the malicious ignoramuses that they are.

No other Republican has ever had the courage to do that. They are all following consultants who warn them not to look unattractively mean-spirited. Don't speak to the people and for Heaven's sake don't listen to them. Give them bromides. Anything else will upset the smooth pursuit of office, the only goal that has ever been sought by Republican "leaders" other than protecting and enhancing wealth. A baker's dozen of Presidential wannabes all spouted identical sales talk.

"Conservative" means nothing to them except a popular advertising slogan. That such people, who don't have a clue as to what "conservative" means, should anathematize Trump as "not a conservative" is ludicrous and illustrates how routinely deceitful the language of American political discourse has become. The only thing worse is giving the definition of "conservative" to the Neocons, aptly dubbed by the author as "semi-repentant communists."

The Republican Establishment has been hysterically upset by unwelcome truths and is busily shooting itself in the foot again and again. An important part of this has been Trump's moderate but effective placing of the guilt for Bush the Lesser's Iraq war, a world-historical blunder, the evil consequences of which will not be escaped by your and my grandchildren. A war that was stupid, dishonestly justified, instigated by a dubious cabal, inappropriate to the provocation that called it forth, and well within the definition of war crime. "The Republican party under Bush did the devil's work," writes Mercer. Who else besides Trump has had the courage to bring forth this necessary dose of reality? And after all we have not been made any safer. The Republican wannabes lined up to tell us the self-evident lie that we will be safer by bringing more Muslims Over Here while dropping more bombs on them Over There.

At a deeper level Trump's discourse has had important effects in making once more respectable the solid, unweasally English language and good old Anglo-Saxon decency and common sense. I admit that Trump's style is not the kind that antiquated Southerners like myself readily warm up to. But I recognize him as an authentic American type with the virtues of the type. If Trump has moral failings in his past life, who of us have not? My support was clinched by his children at the Cleveland convention. You can't fake your children. When have we ever seen such an outstanding brood of potential White House children? In intellect and morals, it seems to me Trump has shown to ability to learn and improve.

"White privilege" and "White Lives Matter Less" have become, in Mercer's words, "the creedal pillar" of our public life. Without ungraciousness to any, Trump has shown that it is OK for white Americans to declare that they have had enough of "the pigment burden" that has been piled on their backs. And this paleo-libertarian author does not disguise her disgust at the fashionable statism, indistinguishable from the collectivist left and without a clue to what "free trade" really means, that passes for libertarianism these days.

The book came out before the Pence nomination. I hoped along with the author that Trump would "go outside the political tribe for a vice president." As far as one can see from the record, Pence is a standard-issue Republican empty suit. We all knew in 1980 that the "Reagan Revolution" was over before it began when Bush *major* was picked as the running mate. We can only hope that Trump knows something that we don't. As president Trump's greatest problem will be covert undermining by the Republican Establishment. He cannot hope to carry out his "revolution" without massive reform in the party itself. After all, these are people who acquiesced in the absurd suppression of the Ten Commandments. And who have spread "the ghastly lie that America is a mere idea" and not a people.

I admit to being green with envy at Mercer's Menckenesque ability to coin memorable labels for the empowered fools of our time. Does any contemporary writer do it better?

Mercer on the media: news nitworks, the War Street Journal, idiot's lantern, unsharpened pencil, tele-tarts, a circle jerk of power brokers, one-trick donkeys, celebrated mediocrities, another banal bloviation, the cable commentariat as a cog in the corpulent D.C. fleshplot, writers who have been amply rewarded for having never written anything remotely original, edgy or interesting.

On our rulers and would-be rulers: parasites in waiting; her doorstopper of a book, nation building at the point of the bayonet makes her barking happy (Hillary); Banana Republicans; dwarf-tossing (William Kristol's promotion of non-entities as Trump alternatives); the quaint expectation that voters, not party operatives, would choose the nominee (anti-Trump machinations of Republican leaders); the silent majority that dare not speak its name; what our crypto-leftist conservatives are ramming down our proverbial gullets are dogmas, not values; master-servant relationship between Republicans and the Religious Right; think tanks' industry for the god of war; neoconservatives speaking like Tocqueville but acting like Robespierre; neoconservatives standing athwart every valid form of American conservatism yelling stop (to play on an old Buckleyism).

When Thomas Jefferson opined that a little rebellion now and then is a good thing he was not speaking as a radical but as a reactionary. With the passage of time, the accumulation of bad precedents, the manipulations of self-seekers, a political society loses focus on its founding ideas. It is necessary for the sound part of the people to *revolve* the system back to its true principles. In that respect, the Trump phenomenon resembles Jeffersonian and Jacksonian democracy—uprisings of the people against a corrupt elite, to break at least temporarily the iron law of oligarchy. As Mercer points out, Trump is strong in almost every cultural region of the country. Where he lacks support is in that widely dispersed cohort of pseudo-intellectuals and trough-feeders that make up a vast part of the American body politic.

Trump, as Mercer points out with tough realism, has only just begun. There is a real question whether there is any longer a "back" to be recovered. In this post-Constitutional time, it may be that "the best liberty lovers can look to is action and counter-action, force and counterforce in the service of liberty." A President hoping for reform will face 160,000 pages of federal laws and regulations and relentless sabotage by the Banksters, Bombers, Bureaucrats, and Busybodies who now govern us. He cannot be a moderate if he hopes to accomplish anything.

In regard to Trump this weary old paleo-conservative agrees with the sprightly young paleo-libertarian writer Mercer on every point. Her endorsement "is not necessarily for the policies of Trump, but for The Process of Trump." At this point, to quibble over the deficiencies of Trump, real or supposed, is like the survivors of the *Titanic* complaining about accommodations on the lifeboats. He is what we have got.

OH DONALD, SAY IT AIN'T SO

BACK WHEN THE REPUBLICAN feedlot was full of wannabes for the next presidential nomination, *Chronicles* web site published my little tongue-in-cheek pieces, "Looking for Mr. Republican" (Sept. 13, 2013) and "Don't Look Any Further, Mr. Republican Has Been Found" (April 3, 2015), describing the ideal Republican candidate. First, he must be presentable and respectable—someone you would consider a good neighbor and who would never violate the standard of American Niceness. He should look presidential, like William McKinley and Warren G. Harding. He must be from north of the Ohio River. He must not have any taint of "extremism," i.e., must never have resisted any leftist pressure. He must be lacking in any ideas or principles, able to smoothly deliver meaningless Republican boilerplate ("compassionate conservatism," "No Child Left Behind," etc.). He must be completely without any intellectual distinction or force of character, either of which might alarm the voters with lack of a moderate and responsible persona. The Republican Party has long specialized in the dumb but nice (Dan Quayle, Bush *minor, ad infinitum*).

Having established all these desirable characteristics, I declared in 2015 that I had found the perfect Mr. Republican: "Pence of Indiana," the perfection of an Establishment Republican empty suit, who had declared himself boldly for "family values" and then run away at the first enemy probe.

Donald Trump has done his country great service by simply telling the truth, tearing a few holes in the great fabric of lies that makes up American public discourse. The American people have responded to his boldness and independence. I believe that I am not alone in fearing that he has now betrayed himself, his cause, and his country by giving in to his discredited Establishment enemies. It is not at all clear that Pence adds any strength to the ticket or to a future administration. He could well prove a bleeding ulcer to Trump. His selection confuses a clear and winning message. Trump should have, if true to himself, chosen a new man—someone young and dynamic and dedicated to destroying Establishment power and obfuscation.

I do not go so far as to think that Trump will be assassinated or impeached, as some have suggested, to make way for a more pliable President, although these things are not entirely beyond possibility. All we can do now is watch and hope.

II. The Republican Charade

LINCOLN AND HIS PARTY

I WANT TO TAKE A LOOK at this strange institution we know as the Republican party and the course of its peculiar history in the American regime. The peculiar history both precedes and continues after Lincoln, although Lincoln is central to the story.

It is fairly easy to construct an ideological account of the Democratic party, what it has stood for and who it has represented, even though there has been at least one revolutionary change during its long history. I generalize broadly, because all major political parties since at least the early 19th century have most of the time sought to dilute their message to broaden their appeal and avoid ideological sharpness. But we can say of the Democratic party that through most of its history it was Jeffersonian—it stood for, at least in lip service, a limited federal government and laissez-faire economy, and it represented farmers and small businessmen, the South, the pioneer West, and to some extent the Northern working class. This identity for the most part even survived the War to Prevent Southern Independence. Clearly, the party in the 20th century came to represent a very different platform—social democracy as defined by the New Deal and the Great Society—and a considerably different constituency. In either case, onlookers have had a pretty good general impression of what the party stood for.

It is nearly impossible to construct a similar description of the Republican party. The party that elected Lincoln was pretty clear about some things, like the tariff, although it may have been less than honest about the reasons. It was obfuscatory about other things. Since Lincoln took power, it has been difficult to find a clear pattern in what the party has claimed to represent. The picture becomes even cloudier when you compare words and behaviour. This, I believe, is because its real agenda has not been such that it could be usefully acknowledged.

Apparently millions continue to harbor the strange delusion that the Republican party is the party of free enterprise, and, at least since the New Deal, the party of conservatism. In fact, the party is and always has been the party of state capitalism. That, along with the powers and perks it provides its leaders, is the whole reason for its creation and continued existence. By state capitalism I mean a regime of highly concentrated private ownership, subsidized and protected by government. The Republican party has never, ever opposed any government interference in the free market or any government expenditure except those that might favour labour unions or threaten Big Business. Consider that for a long time it was the party of high tariffs—when high tariffs benefited Northern big capital and oppressed the South and most of the population. Now it is the party of so-called "free trade"—because that is the policy that benefits Northern big capital, whatever it might cost the rest of us. In succession, Republicans presented opposite policies idealistically as good for America, while carefully avoiding discussion of exactly who it was good for.

There is nothing particularly surprising that there should be a party of state capitalism in the United States. And certainly nothing surprising in the necessity for such a party to present itself as something else. Put in terms the Founding Fathers would have understood, the interests Republicans serve are merely the court party—what Jefferson referred to as the tinsel aristocracy and John Taylor as the paper aristocracy. The American Revolution was a revolt of the country against the court. Jeffersonians understood that every political system divides between the great mass of unorganized folks who mind their own business—that, is, the country party — and the minority who hang around the court to manipulate the government finances and engineer government favours. It is much easier and quicker to get rich by finding a way into the treasury than by hard work. That is mostly what politics is about. Of course, schemes to plunder society through the government must never be seen as such. They must be powdered and perfumed to look like a public good.

Contrary to what we might hope, there was nothing in the New World to inhibit the formation of a court party. In fact, the immense riches of an undeveloped continent merely increased incentives for courtiers. The number of projects that could be imagined as worthy of government support was infinite. In America there were not even any firmly established institutions of credit and currency, control of which was always the quickest route to big riches. Neither was there anything in a democratic system to inhibit state capitalism. The great mass of the citizens could usually be circumvented by people whose fulltime job was lining their pockets by swindling the voters. Lincoln's triumph is most realistically seen as the permanent victory of the court party, a victory that had been sought ever since Alexander Hamilton. The Lincoln regime eliminated all barriers to making the federal government into a machine to transfer money to those interests the party represented (and as many others as needed to be paid off to support the operation).

Hamilton had justified the government enriching his friends at no risk to themselves because "a public debt is a public blessing." The Whigs sometimes argued that the paper issued by their banks was "the people's money" and therefore morally superior as a currency to "government money." Lincoln presented himself as a candidate for the presidency with the slogan "Vote Yourself a Farm!" Once the obstructionism of those troublesome Southerners was broken, ordinary folks could get themselves a farm for free out of the public lands. Some ordinary folks did get land—but most of the free land, millions of acres, went to government-connected corporations. Saving the Union, freeing the slaves but keeping them out of the North, and giving opportunity to the common people, when filtered through Lincoln's masterful rhetoric, gave the party of Big Business a lock on the righteous vote for a long time to come.

The most consistent aspect of Republican party has been its role as the respectable party, without much attention to principles and policies. Its voters have been those who think of themselves as more respectable and more patriotic than the voters of the other party. What I am trying to describe is captured by the pejorative label the Republicans long used for their Democratic opponents. The Democrats were said to be the party of "Rum, Romanism, and Rebellion," that is, of wastrels, Catholics, and Southerners. The bloody shirt was waved through decades in which the party definitely had an agenda, but one which was not described too frankly. There are plenty of good reasons for disliking liberals, but when the current Republican radio demagogues anathematize liberals they are merely appealing to the same vague feelings of superior virtue that fueled "Rum, Romanism, and Rebellion." The one attitude that Republicans have most consistently displayed is disdain for the South, because such an attitude has been always highly respectable and was the basis of their first rise to power. In their platform of 1900 they justified the slaughter then going on in the Philippines by likening the rebels there to the Southern traitors of earlier times who deserved death for the evil deed of resisting the best government on earth. Very recently, the national chairman of the Republican party went before a civil rights group to apologize for that party's "Southern strategy." As far as I know he did not repudiate the seven out of the last ten national elections that were won by that strategy.

The Republican party has had to live with a large gap between what it says and what it does. Deceit has become a habit and a fixed policy. Republican leaders always, and I mean always, act as if truth is the worst possible strategy— always opt for the gimmick instead of straight talk. Richard Nixon—like Lincoln a crackpot realist—thought only of damage control when simple truth-telling might have saved him. It might occur to some observers that the crackpot realist mode describes pretty well the way a recent war was started and carried on. What I am trying to describe here is something more than the usual elasticity of politicians who lie as a tool of the trade. When Charles Beard's *An Economic Interpretation of the Constitution of the United States* was published, suggesting that theretofore unseen profit-seeking had had a major role in the creation of the U.S. Constitution, Republican President William Howard Taft is said to have commented that what Beard wrote was true but it should not have been told to the public.

The very name of the Republican party is a lie. The name was chosen when the party formed in the 1850s to suggest a likeness to the Jeffersonian Republicans of earlier history. This had a very slender plausibility. One of the main goals of the new party was "free soil"—preventing slavery (and Negroes) from existence in any territories, that is, future states.

It is quite true that in the 1780s Jefferson, and indeed most Southerners, had voted to exclude slavery from the Northwest Territory—what became the

Midwest, a region to which Virginia had by far the strongest claim by both charter and conquest. However, the sentiments and reasoning that supported that restriction were very different from those of the Republican Free-Soilers of the 1850s.

To detect the lie, all you have to do is look at the stance of Jefferson himself and most of his followers, Northern and Southern, in the Missouri controversy of 1819 - 1820. The effort to eliminate slavery from Missouri and all the territories, the first version of Lincoln's free-soil policy, was denounced by Jefferson as a threat to the future of the Union and a transparent Northern power grab. It was "the fire-bell in the night." In the 1780s the foreign slave trade was still open. In 1819 no more slaves were being imported and the black population was increasing naturally in North America at a greater rate than anywhere else in the world (as it always has). At that point, Jefferson said, the best course for the eventual elimination of slavery was not to restrict it but to disperse it as thinly as possible.

The Southern Republicans who had criticized and sought to restrict slavery in the 1780s had in mind the long-term welfare of all Americans. The Northern Republicans of the 1850s who raised a truly hysterical and exaggerated campaign against what they called "the spread of slavery" were entirely different people with entirely different motives. Not even to mention, of course, that the Northern Republicans were totally committed to a mercantilist agenda, every plank of which Jeffersonians had defined themselves by being against. The Republicans of the 1850s exactly represented those parts of the country and those interests that had been the most rabid opponents of Jefferson and his Republicans. (Interestingly, the areas of the country today that are the most liberal—the northeast, upper Midwest, and west coast, are exactly the areas that from the 1850s to the 1930s were the most solidly Republican— and "respectable." (Old-fashioned Democrats used to say that the change from a small government party to a leftist one was a take-over of the Democrats by Republican Progressives.)

In 1860 the Republicans promoted their candidate as the "rail-splitter," the poor boy who had made good, an example and representative of the "common people." This image, of course, had nothing to do with the Lincoln of 1860, with his agenda, or with the important issues of the time. This was not new. It was a mimicry of the Whig campaign of 1840. For a long time, our New England-dominated history books have portrayed the election of the natural aristocrat Andrew Jackson in 1828 as beginning a vulgarization of American politics. But it was actually the Whig campaign of 1840 that successfully pioneered the transformation of national political campaigns into mindless mass celebrations. It showed how it is done. The party did not trouble itself to adopt a platform nor to nominate for President any of its well-known leaders. It put up the elderly General Harrison of Ohio, who had been a hero in the War of 1812 and a senator and governor some time back. General Harrison entertained company but issued no position papers. His candidacy was promoted by a slogan "Tippecanoe and Tyler Too" and by mass torchlight parades and rallies featuring the log cabin in which Harrison supposedly lived, the coonskin cap he supposedly wore, and the jug of home-distilled from which he supposedly sipped. The general actually lived on quite a considerable estate near Cincinnati and was a Virginia aristocrat by birth. In fact, he and his running mate, John Tyler, had both been born in the same small county in Tidewater Virginia—Charles City County (which was a part of my rookie news reporter's beat long ago and far away in my misspent youth).

As a further obfuscation, Tyler had been added to the ticket to appeal to Southerners who were opposing the controlling Van Buren Democrats for quite different reasons than were the Whigs. Harrison swept the Middle States and Midwest, though his victory probably owed as much to a bad economy and Van Buren's lack of appeal as to the Whig campaign. Immediately Henry Clay, hero and Congressional leader of the Whigs, announced that the election was a mandate for the Whig program—raising the tariff up again, re-establishing the national bank, and distributing lavishly from the treasury to companies that promised to build infrastructure. All this, although the issues had never been set forth in a platform nor mentioned in the campaign. Remind you of any more recent Presidential mandates for things that were never discussed before the voters?

The "log cabin" gambit has been used and re-used as when the Wall Street lawyer Wendell Wilkie was promoted as a simple Hoosier country lad, and two rich Connecticut candidates were marketed as "good ole boys" from Texas.

Let's look at Lincoln's party as it was born in the 1850s. In March of 1850, William H. Seward, the chief architect of the Republican party and its foremost spokesman until Lincoln maneuvered him out of the Presidential nomination, made a speech against compromise, anticipating his later famous remarks: "the irrepressible conflict" between the North and the South. This speech was not a somber warning about impending trouble as is usually assumed. It was a celebration of the coming certain triumph of the North over the South. James K. Paulding, New York man of letters and former Secretary of the Navy under Van Buren, wrote about Seward's oration:

"I cannot express the contempt and disgust with which I have read the speech of our Senator Seward, though it is just what I expected from him. He is one of the most dangerous insects that ever crawled about in the political atmosphere, for he is held in such utter contempt by all honest men that no notice is taken of him till his sting is felt. He is only qualified to play the most despicable parts in the political drama, and the only possible way he can acquire distinction is by becoming the tool of greater scoundrels than himself. Some years ago, after disgracing the State of New York as Chief Magistrate, he found his level in the lowest depths of insignificance and oblivion, and was dropped by his own party. But the mud was stirred at the very bottom of the pool, and he who went down a mutilated tadpole has come up a full-grown bull frog, more noisy and impudent than ever. This is very often the case among us here, where nothing is more common than to see a swindling rogue, after his crimes have been a little rusted by time, suddenly become an object of public favour or executive patronage. The position taken and the principles asserted by this pettifogging rogue in his speech would disgrace any man—but himself."

Paulding adds: "I fear it will not be long before we of the North become the tools of the descendants of the old Puritans . . . .": He means that the well-known and much despised New England fanaticism was encroaching upon the whole North.

This is one Northern commentary on the origins of the Republican party and on the sad public conditions that made it possible. Failed politicians of both parties, like Lincoln, had seized the occasion of the acquisition of new territory from Mexico to launch themselves forward in a way destructive of the comity of the Union. The opportunity they made the most of had two parts: the discontent of major Northern economic interests over free trade and separation of the government from control of the bankers that had been accomplished by the Democrats; and the hysterical and false claims that Southerners were conspiring to spread slavery to the North, given plausibility by three decades of vicious vituperation against the South. The Republican success depended on a Northern public that was unsettled by economic change, religious ferment, and immigration. Thus these politicians were able to form for the first time in American history a purely sectional party, something that every patriot had warned against.

Almost all current interpretations of the meaning of the Republican war against the South 1861 - 1865 come to rest on pretty phrases from Lincoln's speeches. If you look at primary sources, as historians used to do, you get a very different picture. In their private letters and sometimes in public speeches the Republican leaders reveal themselves to be just the ruthless villains that several previous generations of historians knew them to be. They boast about their intention to keep control of the government by any means, to keep the South captive for economic exploitation, sometimes about their intent to exterminate the Southern people. (Those in favour of the last-mentioned are usually clergymen.) They revel triumphantly in conquest in a manner that puts one in mind of Nazis. As for the glory of emancipation that so long lent righteousness to their war, as Frederick Douglass pointed out, Lincoln's party was pre-eminently the party of white men. Before, during, and after the war the Republicans never did anything with a primary motive of the welfare of the black people. The black people were for use for higher purposes, for keeping down the South and keeping the Republicans in power. Most importantly, they were to stay in the South. Millions of acres of vacant western land could be given away to corporations who could provide the representatives of the people with the proper cash incentives, but there was not a patch for the freedmen.

In the free-soil debates before the war Republican leaders dwell not on the evil of slavery but on their intention to keep the black scourge out of the new territories, which must be reserved for white men only. Senator Benjamin Wade of Ohio, stalwart Radical Republican, writes his wife that he hates to go to Washington because of all the n-words there. If you look at the iconography of Emancipation, what you see is not a celebration of black freedom but a celebration of Northern nobility of which the blacks are the passive and slavishly grateful beneficiaries.

What other elements besides opportunistic politicians went into making this new party? Obviously the powers of industry and finance that would know how to profit from a new regime. And the New England intelligentsia for whom, by common consent, we can cite Ralph Waldo Emerson as the representative. Emerson who said he was more concerned about one white men corrupted by slavery than about a thousand enslaved blacks; who also said that the inhabitants of the Massachusetts penitentiary were superior to the leaders of the South; and that serial killer John Brown was a great man.

Another major ingredient in the Republican confection were the nativists formerly of the American party. Lincoln was too shrewd to come right out as a nativist, but he gladly accepted the support of the people who had torched convents in Boston and Philadelphia. It is not very well known that nativist vigilantes called "Wide-Awakes" carried out mob action against enemies of the Republican party before and during the war. And you thought only Southerners were guilty of mob violence.

Another founding block of the Republican party, often overlooked, were German refugees from the 1848 revolutions. Their numbers in the Midwest, as much as fifteen per cent of the population in some states, were great enough to form a major voting block and to account for the change of the Midwest from Democrat to Republican between 1850 and 1860. In other words, there were just as many state rights democrats in the Midwest in 1860 as there had been in

1850, but they could now be outvoted. Lincoln cultivated this cohort early by secretly subsidizing its newspapers and involving its leaders as activists in his behalf. For the new Germans the predominant nativist Puritans of the North made an exception to their dislike of all non-Anglo-Saxons. In the German revolutionaries they found spiritual kinsmen.

Pre-1848 German immigrants, German Catholics, and those belonging to quieter Protestant sects did not participate in Republican fervor. Let's understand who these German Republicans were. They were military nationalists. You can call them proto-communist or proto-fascist, it doesn't matter. It amounts to the same thing. When the foremost among them, Carl Schurz, arrived in America he complained that the Americans were too laid-back and unideological in their politics and he vowed to change that. These Germans believed that the unified and aggressive nation-state was the height of human existence, that progress toward it was inevitable, and that obstacles to centralization and revolution should be violently destroyed like the provincial aristocracies and petty princes of Europe. These Germans were among the most active and aggressive of Republican orators and campaigners and motivated Union soldiers. Before they arrived, America had been marked by a regional conflict between Northerners and Southerners with contradictory interests and inclinations. With the rise to influence of the Forty-Eighters the manageable competition of different regions became in the Northern mind an ideological class conflict.

On one side was Freedom and the nation. On the other side an evil force called the Slave Power, a deadly enemy that must be destroyed like any other obstacle to the ascent of the nation toward perfection.

So that, as he records in his memoirs, General Richard Taylor of the Confederate Army, son of a President of the United States and grandson of a Revolutionary officer, when he surrendered in 1865, was lectured by a German in a federal general's uniform about how Southerners were now going to be forced to learn the true principles of America. (I always think of the "scholarship" of Harry Jaffa when I recall this incident.)

Let us always come back to the fundamentals. The Republican party engineered and carried out a bloody war against Americans that revolutionized the basis on which our liberty had been built. They maintained a cold war for another decade, governing by force and fraud, unprecedented in American history. While in power they bribed, swindled and looted themselves to private wealth that still underpins many fortunes. Historians of the first half of the twentieth century, whether liberals or conservatives, read the sources and understood this. They regarded what had occurred as a great national tragedy. But now it is all rendered in Marxist terms (whether those who are following the line realize it or not) as a great revolution that unfortunately failed to go far enough. Historians now see nothing in the experience but the race question. They condemn the evil Southerners who sometimes intimidated black voters in attempting to bring about an end to the disorder and blatant "legal" stealing of Reconstruction. That during Republican rule there had been pervasive fraud and terror and never an honest election in the occupied territories is not worth mentioning.

I doubt if even Lincoln and his stoutest supporters would agree that their pursuit of power and profit amounted to an unfortunately incomplete Marxist revolution. That was not exactly what they had in mind.

DEMOCRATS AND REPUBLICANS

EARNEST READERS WANT to know what the difference is between the two major political parties. I have tried to provide some helpful guidance.

DEMOCRAT. Someone who believes that when people who have enjoyed a wealthy life but behaved badly get into trouble they should be rescued by non-wealthy people who have worked hard and played by the rules.

REPUBLICAN. Someone who believes that when people who have enjoyed a wealthy life but behaved badly get into trouble they should be rescued by non-wealthy people who have worked hard and played by the rules.

* * *

DEMOCRAT. Someone who thinks it is good to disinherit posterity and turn the country over to the wretched refuse of the earth.

REPUBLICAN. Someone who thinks it is good to disinherit posterity and turn the country over to the wretched refuse of the earth—as long as he can turn a short-term profit.

* * *

DEMOCRAT. Someone who thinks the U.S. has a right to invade any and every country to impose feminism and multiculturalism.

REPUBLICAN. Someone who thinks the U.S. has a right to invade any and every country to impose feminism and multiculturalism and to get some payback—whether that particularly county has done us any harm or not and as long as the right people make some money.

* * *

DEMOCRAT. Someone who sees the future as an egalitarian, multicultural paradise for all humanity.

REPUBLICAN. Someone who sees the future as an egalitarian, multicultural paradise with technological wonders and high profits.

* * *

DEMOCRAT. Someone who thinks that the Supreme Court is the instrument to impose progressive policies on a reluctant public.

REPUBLICAN. Someone who thinks the Supreme Court is the instrument to impose one-man rule, as long as Republicans are in power.

* * *

DEMOCRAT. Someone who thinks abortion is a good thing.

REPUBLICAN. Someone who doesn't care about abortion but has been told that saying you are against it gets votes.

* * *

DEMOCRAT. Someone who thinks the purpose of government is to provide welfare for bureaucrats, minority groups, and rich people.

REPUBLICAN. Someone who thinks the purpose of government is to provide welfare for rich people, bureaucrats' and minority groups.

* * *

DEMOCRAT. Someone who hopes that if you push affirmative action for everything you will eventually get an affirmative action President.

REPUBLICAN. Someone who can't figure out that if you push affirmative-action for everything you will eventually get an affirmative-action President.

ELECTION EXPLAINED (2012)

Reasons for voting Democrat:

More freebies, welfare, government jobs, grants; satisfaction of leftist ideological malice; if you are a minority, the pleasure of sticking it to Whitey.

Reasons for voting Republican:

Unless you are a big capitalist, a defense contractor, an employer of illegal immigrants, or a politician hoping for the perks of office, there are none.*

*Historical note: The Republican party prospered pretty well for a century and a half by never doing anything for its voters except giving them a sense of respectability, of superiority to the immigrant herd and Southern barbarians. But now, except in the clueless boondocks, it is more respectable to be a Democrat. (Some people have voted Republican in the hope of slowing down the Democrat destruction of the country, but they have been and are certain to continue to be disappointed. To keep doing the same thing over and over although it never works is one of the definitions of insanity. However, in this case it is not so much insanity as desperation and inability to think outside the box.)

A REPUBLICAN IS SOMEONE WHO THINKS

. . . .

—THAT UNEMPLOYMENT COMPENSATION for laid-off workers is socialism and multi-billion dollar bailouts for banking and stock swindlers is capitalism.

—That killing women and children with high explosives in remote corners of the earth is "defending our way of life."

—That the purpose of education is to train good workers.

—That immigration is good because it supplies good cheap workers.

—That Earl Warren, Nelson Rockefeller, Gerald Ford, George W. Bush, Newt Gingrich, Rudy Giuliani, Colin Powell, Mitt Romney, and Paul Ryan are great American statesmen.

—That the main reason not to train women for combat is that it is inefficient.

—That the 10th Amendment means that the federal government should tell the States what to do rather than do it itself.

—That criticism of Lincoln is near treason.

—That the President is "Commander-in-Chief" of the country, especially when he is a Republican.

—That freedom is protected by undeclared wars and military tribunals.

—That "right to life" is a good campaign gimmick, but not to be taken seriously.

—That any campaign promise or slogan should gull the saps who are not in the know but is not to be taken seriously.

—That the way to beat the Democrats is to take up whatever they propose and promise to do it better.

LOOKING FOR MR. REPUBLICAN

PREVIOUSLY, I IMPERTINENTLY SUGGESTED a revision to Sam Francis's brilliant and justly famous description of the Republicans as "the stupid party." Republicans always abandon their positions and surrender to the enemy. This behavior is presumably stupid because it damages and weakens the party by betraying its base.

Matters become clearer when we realize that the Republican party is not a political party. A political party may indulge in evasion and compromise, but by definition it represents some real and substantial interests in society and some shared ideas about what constitutes the public good. The Republican party does not meet this definition. It is not a party but a sales organization—and what could be more American than that? Its function is to promote men, usually well-to-do, who have no ideas and represent nothing but themselves, but are ambitious for the rewards of power—the satisfaction of vanity, greed, and lust.

As is to be expected in an organization devoted to selling products, all the instincts of such men are commercial rather than political. They avoid confrontation and dogma, which would be taken by too many Americans as not nice and because they really have nothing to argue for. Debate and deliberation, which are the soul of democratic government, do not exist in national politics, largely thanks to the Republicans, for the Democrats, "the evil party," do have a real constituency and ideology. Corporate managers do not argue with their accusers over facts and values—they launch an ad campaign to convey a likable image, insubstantial as that image may be in terms of ideas and principles.

This is particularly so today when corporate power is dominated, not by entrepreneurs and producers, but by men who inherited their position or who manipulated and cheated their way up the ladder of a bureaucracy. Think of the "leaders" the Republican party has foisted on the country in the last few decades: Nelson Rockefeller, Dan Quayle, Gerald Ford, Kemp, the two Bushes, the two Romneys, Rice, Rumsfeld, Powell, *ad infinitum*. All people with no real accomplishments, of mediocre intellect, and with no ideas except what seem to be popular at the time. Intelligence is not everything—character is perhaps more important. But a dumb person of good character may be too easily misled as to what is good and bad and the Republican party specializes in the dumb but nice. But what could be more American than that?

CONSERVATISM WITHOUT ALEXANDER, ABRAHAM, OR IRVING

BRION MCCLANAHAN, one of the best young historians of the day, and I have collaborated on a book: *Forgotten Conservatives in American History*. Before you are off-put by the reference to "conservatives" in the title, consider some of the sixteen figures we have treated – John Taylor of Caroline, Condy Raguet, Grover Cleveland, William Graham Sumner. Our goal has been to establish a conservative tradition of thought that, from the War of Independence to the later 20th century, defended the decentralist, laissez-faire, and non-interventionist regime bequeathed by the best of the Founding Fathers. The true conservatives have been those who wanted to let the American people alone and not hector and dragoon them into schemes of "progress" and foreign entanglement.

Conservatism, for us, has been a powerful and eloquent train of thinkers who have opposed the Hamilton/Lincoln regime of state-capitalism and the Roosevelt/Bush/Obama agenda of "global democracy." Our conservatism stands strongly contra to the historic Republican party and to "neoconservative" imperialism. In this we are not so much out-of-step as some may think. Russell Kirk, "the father of modern conservatism," considered Alexander Hamilton to be no conservative but rather a dubious "innovator." And more than once Kirk lamented that "the conservative disposition" in the United States has too often been misunderstood by identifying it with rent-seeking behaviour.

As we have tried to show, many of the great figures of American literature—James Fenimore Cooper, H.L. Mencken, William Faulkner—fit well into our scheme of true American conservatism. The thinkers Dr. McClanahan and I have presented are perhaps not so much forgotten as they are unheeded, but they are all good men who have warned tellingly of the march toward the regime of regimentation and exploitation that is now established. Not only established but celebrated as the glorious end of history.

The likenesses between Neocons and Nazis: the same worship of force and equation of force with morality; the same disdain for other people's ideas and interests and presumption of special and superior vision; the same contempt for law, tradition, and the opinion of the civilized world; the same forced redefinition of history according to a European ideology; the same racialist disdain for the inferior breeds; the same manipulation of the public with exaggerated and misplaced fears; the same reliance on propaganda slogans and disregard of truth; the same preference for the Leader over democratic process; the same boastful launching of illegal wars of aggression; the same blundering in military action and occupation.

Neocons have a point when they claim the mantle of Lincoln. Such is the hold of Lincoln's fraudulent sainthood on the American consciousness that many people, especially liberals, are deeply offended at having Bush likened to Lincoln. Granted: Unlike the Bush boy, Lincoln was intelligent, literate, professionally successful, and a shrewd politician who manipulated others rather than being manipulated by them. But their presidencies do bear a strong family resemblance: launching of an unnecessary war of aggression, a war largely fueled by greed, government-worship, and the blasphemous equation of God and America; repeated miscalculations in the conduct of the war; disregard for the lives and property of civilians; evasion and misrepresentation of constitutional limitations and abuse of civil liberties; a giant step toward transforming the republican United States into an empire.

Allowing that the 19th century had not perfected the instruments of totalitarianism that we now enjoy, perhaps we should admit that Junior Bush is merely fulfilling an American tradition.

THE DISAPPEARANCE OF CONSERVATISM
(1992)

THE DEFEAT AND DISAPPEARANCE of what has been known as conservatism in the 20th century is a subject worthy of a large book. What would be said in such a book would depend on whether we took a historical focus of a few years, a few decades, or a larger span. And on whether we looked at political parties and mass politics, intellectual movements, or far-reaching social change.

It is possible that the most recent American experience in international adventurism has effectively finished off what we have known as conservatism, and also what has been known as liberalism—both swallowed up by the imperial state, for which ideas. principles, and even material interests are expendable. For the massive military intervention in the Middle East, unlike earlier ones, has not occurred because of unavoidable conflict, but by deliberate choice. It has no measurable goal or termination and has caused rather than settled conflict.

It would be interesting to pursue Roman analogies and what they suggest about the long-term perils of bankruptcy and proletarianisation for the state that undertakes the imperial role. But it is perhaps enough to point out that the bill is not in for the economic and psychic costs, and they cannot be discussed until the present euphoria has passed. And that politicians will be able to obfuscate the costs for a long time.

It would also be interesting to chart the course of movement of intellectual conservatism into the terminal state of vulgarity and triviality in which George Will can be regarded as a leading intellectual. However, I will focus in this brief space on the strange and almost unnoticed failure and betrayal of conservatism as a domestic political movement, despite three resounding national election victories.

The chief reason for this failure is that conservatism allowed itself to be captured within the contaminated vessel of the Republican Party. Bush *major*, who was elected three times on an anti-affirmative action platform, is for affirmative action. And who can gainsay the Great Emancipator of Kuwait? He was elected by millions concerned about the Willie Hortons of the world. We have no evidence that he has done anything about the Willie Hortons. We have no evidence that he wishes to do anything. The only evidence we have is that he wants the votes of those who are concerned.

He was elected, after an explicit promise, by the votes of millions of middle and working-class Americans who sought some remedy for the government burden on their earnings. They now face increased government spending and greater taxes, to bailout the bureaucracy, the bankers, and the sheiks. Northeastern yuppies who voted for Dukakis may take a tax deduction for the interest on their vacation homes. The millions of middle-class people who voted for Bush cannot take a deduction for the interest paid to buy a car needed to get to work and support the government.

The difference between the Democratic and Republican parties—and this dichotomy can be found in earlier periods of the history of the vile American two-party system—is that the Democrats serve their constituency. The unions. minority groups, bureaucrats, and assorted social enemies who support them can expect to profit by their victory. And also by their defeat, since the other party neither wants to nor can provide effective opposition to their agenda.

The Republicans have been talking about the Emerging Republican Majority, Middle America, the Silent Majority, etc. for more than two decades now. Some pundits have wondered why this Majority has not emerged. The explanation is simple. It has been betrayed by the Republican Party, which wants its votes but not its platform. The only effective conservative movement in recent history in mass politics was that of a non-Republican, George Wallace, which made a far profounder change in American politics than the so-called Reagan Revolution. If Wallace had not badly scared the leaders of both parties, they would not now be giving even lip service to the concerns of

Middle America. The function of the Republican Party is to capture and contain those concerns.

Many political movements and tendencies emerged in postwar America--those of Johnson, Nixon, Wallace, Reagan, and others. But the winner has been that tendency that had the least popular support: Nelson Rockefeller's. His Liberal Republicanism of the 1960s postulated that the Republicans could do everything the Democrats could do, but could do it better. (Meanwhile minimising impact on the inherited wealth of the Northeast.) Thanks to the nature and history of the Republican Party, despite unfailing rejection at the polls, that regime is now triumphant.

A Cheer and a Half for Democrats

"God is a Radical [Republican], and the devil is a conservative."
—The Rev. Henry Ward Beecher, 1866

"God is Pro-War."
—The Rev. Jerry Falwell, 2005

LONG AGO IN OUR CALLOW DAYS we thought that American conservatism was the Christian social philosophy of Russell Kirk and Richard Weaver. We did not know that American conservatism was really Trotskyites, oil barons, Likudniks, Dr. Strangeloves, amoral political technicians, fringe Protestant loonies, and ignorant, vulgar media demagogues. We should have known. In retrospect, it was inevitable, given the quality of the human material available in the Republican Party.

I thought "the Talent on Loan from God" with the Golden Microphone and Bully O'Reilly could not be topped among the media demagogues until my local station started putting on someone named Glen Beck after the news. Mr. Beck opined that he was not opposed to the new Muslim congressman taking his oath on the Koran, because people will be more trustworthy if they swear on what they believe in. He thinks they should swear the oath on *Playboy* if that is what they believe in. Mr. Beck, the great conservative spokesperson, apparently does not know the origin and meaning of oaths in the civilization that he was nominally born into. The same fellow further contributed to the enlightenment of national discourse by declaring President Carter "an idiot."

Bill Clinton is no saint, but he did reduce the debt, reform welfare, and avoid losing wars. These accomplishments are doubtless less substantial than they seem. But no Republican President in the last half century has even come close.

How sweet is the triumph of conservatism!

SAVE AMERICA: VOTE REPUBLICAN IN 2004

THE WORLD'S PRESS seems to have discovered the neocons and fingered them as the villains in America's great leap into imperial decadence by its pre-emptive war against Iraq. This belated revelation brings only a wry and sad satisfaction to some of us who have been warning the commonwealth about this nasty little cabal for well over twenty years now. (There is nothing less rewarding than being right too soon. Look what happened to Cassandra.)

Nevertheless, I wonder if the "Blame the Neocons" chorus hasn't become as excessive as it is belated and repetitive—a diversion from more fundamental problems. These people have never received a single vote in any election. They are courtiers who owe all their power to manipulation of people who have been voted for. The Neocons are opportunists of power. Opportunists go where there is opportunity. Who gave them the opportunity to pursue an agenda that has never been presented honestly to the people?

While their power seems to have become particularly apparent lately in foreign affairs, there is nothing new about it. It has been there since Reagan took office, when Neocon gophers like Bill Bennett took over all the cultural and educational functions of the federal government. It was startlingly evident when Vice President Dan Quayle was appointed gopher to Neocon Bill Kristol.

Could it be that the neocons are not the problem, but merely a symptom of the problem? Would they even exist in their present form if they had not seen the chance presented by the vast gaping vacuum of ideas and principles that is the Republican Party, and particularly its current leader?

Think back to 2000, when "conservative" spokesmen, some of whom were honest people who should have known better, exhorted us that we must vote for Bush, even if we had to hold our nose. The alternative was unthinkable! The

Democrats might get in! Then we would have abortion, gay rights, affirmative action, judicial tyranny, socialized medicine, needless foreign war, massive spending, deficits, and debt! Save what is left of America! Vote Republican! Yeah, right.

I often raised objections in conversation to this exhortation. What reason did we have to think that George W. Bush would avert all those disasters? Exactly none. The evidence was all the other way—massively and conclusively. The best response I ever got from the reluctant Bush warriors (which I still hear all the time) was "at least Bush is a good Christian man" who would cleanse the White House of the sewage left behind by the long incumbency of Clinton. As if Bush were running against Clinton rather than Gore. This about a man who professed a shallow, carnival-tent version of Christianity. A Christian who has subsequently altered the American creed of "Protestant, Catholic, and Jew" to "Protestant, Catholic, Jew, and Muslim." And given his stand on immigration, we will soon have Santeria and Hinduism added.

It seems to come down to this: Bush was elected (sort of) because of name recognition (son of a former, if failed, President) and because he seemed less depraved than Clinton.

What did we know for certain about George W. Bush in 2000?

We knew that he was not very bright, guaranteeing that as President he would be managed by others more intelligent. He seldom spoke coherently and had never expressed a thought that was other than a slogan or showed even a normal, every-day moral and intellectual maturity.

Intellect is not everything. Character is vital. Who knew it and when did they know it, as repentant Communists used to ask? What did we know about Bush's character in 2000? An under-achieving rich boy who, as far as one could tell, had never done a day's work in the real world or dealt with a real-world hardship in his life. An alcoholic who had shirked his military duties. A moral adolescent who smirked and snickered over the grave matter of capital punishment.

But, after all, he was a successful "conservative" governor, wasn't he? Knowledgeable conservatives in Texas told us that as governor he had shunned conservatives at every turn and collaborated with the left on every spending and social issue. He was enthusiastic for affirmative action and the Mexification of the country. Whatever the Republican platform might say, and he repudiated that even before his formal nomination. There was not the tiniest reason to hope that the son of "Read My Lips" would do anything other than betray conservatives on every social issue. It was blatantly plain to all but liars and the willfully blind that his campaign statements were not expressions of belief or intent but merely stunts to gull a segment of the voters. Looking carefully, you could find no principle and only one large-scope policy proposal in his campaign for the seat of George Washington—that great conservative desideratum: nationalization of education!

No one in American history can more truly be said to have bought the office of President. His campaign chest, not his popularity, bought a quick nomination. The Republican convention of 2000 was not a convention—it was an infomercial. Not a single unpackaged idea appeared. Not a single real issue was debated or even mentioned. In fact, any member of the party who threatened to utter an unapproved thought was literally barred from the platform in favor of endless boilerplate from media-approved celebrities. A travesty on the very essence of government of the people and a relay station on the road to emperor worship.

Then there was the election, which the Democrats tried to steal by a transparent fraud over a few votes in Florida. The conservative (i.e., honest) response to this would be to point out that the Democrats got as close as they did only because they had voted felons and aliens, bribed black preachers to get out the vote (something they learned from Reconstruction Republicans), and committed all their other usual felonies. That would have been a healthy dose of realism, but far too honest and forthright for Republicans. The proper authority, the state legislature, should have settled the disputed election. Instead, the Bushies ran to the most arbitrary and centralized power they could find, the Supreme Court, providing new validation for judicial activism and leaving the charge of a stolen Presidency hanging in the air. All that counted was grabbing the office. The democratic integrity of the process was of no interest even when it was on their side.

Bush voters are now complaining about his appointments—the evils perpetrated by Rumsfeld, Wolfowitz, Ashcroft, Perle, etc. But why should they be surprised? There has been no unexpected coup. Neocons like Rumsfeld and Wolfowitz have impeccable credentials as Republican appointees going back to Reagan. As for Ashcroft and his zealous pursuit of a police state, why he is just a standard-issue Republican politico, interchangeable with several dozen other governors and congressmen. Substitute any of them for Ashcroft and they would still be supporting "my President" in all. For that matter, why should anyone who has ever heard of Edwin M. Stanton, William H. Seward, Earl Warren, or Thaddeus Stevens be surprised at Republican indifference to individual liberty?

For that matter, there is nothing in Bush's action and rhetoric of benevolent aggression that is radically incompatible with the tradition of Lincoln, Theodore Roosevelt, Nixon, Reagan, or Bush the Previous, who declared himself to be Prince of The New World Order.

Hard leftists understood the neocons from the beginning and dismissed them contemptuously as opportunists. Some of the leftists are intelligent and realistic about power. So the neocons had to go where there were "leaders" vacuous enough to regard them as brilliant thinkers and policy architects. Taking over the Republican "leaders" was child's play. The Republicans have always had a liking for empty brains behind pretty faces. We are talking here about the party of such intellectual giants as William McKinley, Warren Harding, Nelson Rockefeller, Dan Quayle, and Jack Kemp. Sam Francis recently wrote that the left preferred the neocons as their official opposition because the neocons are not really conservative. True. They also prefer them because they are either mentally challenged or conspicuously unattractive, unlike, say, Ronald Reagan or Pat Buchanan.

The leftists have made some cogent criticisms of Bush imperialism, but I wish they would stop attributing his sins to his being a Christian and a Texan.

The Republican religious right has nothing to do with Christianity and Bush is no more a Texan than Hillary Clinton is from Arkansas, even if his fellow Yalies made him feel less than a true blue Yankee because his family had emigrated to the colonies. Thinking that God has chosen you to make war to purify the world is pure Connecticut, as is making a show of it. We are talking here about Connecticut's two greatest contributions to American culture—John Brown and P.T. Barnum. Not that Texans don't have their own faults to answer for. Lyndon Johnson probably did more irreparable damage to our country than even Lincoln or Roosevelt, or anybody before George W.

Why do people who should know better keep invoking the strange fallacy that to choose a Republican over a Democrat is to strike a blow for conservatism? The Republican Party came to power in a Jacobin revolution, implemented by the wholesale murder of dissenting Americans. Its "conservatism" has always consisted of support for one version of "capitalism"—not free markets and free enterprise but private ownership with government subsidy. The only government involvement in the economy it has ever opposed is that of which favored corporations disapproved.

And it has always covered up that real agenda with appeals to the respectable but not too bright part of the population, marketed in demagogic packaging that pointed to the alleged evils of its opponents: "Rum, Romanism, and Rebellion," i.e., the perils presented by un-American Catholics and Southerners; or made claims to be the keeper of prosperity: "Vote Yourself a Farm" (Lincoln), or "A Chicken in Every Pot" (Hoover). Millions of people were apparently convinced that being against Clinton was the same thing as being in favor of something worthwhile.

There are, of course, some actual conservatives in the Republican Party, mainly in the House of Representatives where the officeholders have to make some connection with real, living constituents. During the 1930s and 1940s, some Republican conservatives, of a breed now nearly extinct, did heroic service opposing the government's plunge into international mayhem. However, they never had sufficient strength to nominate a presidential candidate or prevent very many evils.

The 1960s saw an upsurge of real conservatism in response to the closely related phenomena of ongoing breakdown of civilization and unbridled expansion of federal greed and power. The consequence of that upsurge was the Goldwater nomination. As with Reagan later, the party tilted in a conservative direction mainly because of the influx of expelled Democrats, like Reagan himself, who had inherited ideas, however attenuated, of such un-Republican things as state's rights and limited government.

But the Republican Establishment made short work of the rebellious canaille who had nominated Goldwater. He was killed off, even before he was nominated, by the "respectable" powers in his own party collaborating with the leftist media to brand him as extremist. The only states he carried were traditionally Democratic ones. The real Republicans never actually lost control of the party. The mantle then fell to Nixon, who, like the Bushes, was compelled to make dishonest and unwelcome conservative noises for one reason and one reason only: because the Democrat George Wallace had brought some genuine issues into the public discourse.

Nostalgists still hearken back to the Reagan Revolution, which never took place except in imagination. The Reagan Revolution was over before the nomination was formalized, when the bankers forced him to accept a "mainstream" Republican on the ticket. The crusade to restrain the federal government, to correct the fraud, incompetence, insolence, and extravagance of its departments, never even got out of port, much less sailed for the Holy Land. And whatever moral capital was left was picked up by the Establishment Republicans once more. Clearly Bush the Previous had no affinity for the social conservatives he had to pretend to care for. Like his son, his instincts on the social questions were pure northeastern Liberal Republican. Previous Bush's Liberal Republican appointee to head the National Endowment of the Arts subsidized Mapplethorpe and the other abominations. Out in the provinces there were many very talented, under-recognized artists who might have been encouraged, some of whom had even voted Republican, but of course they were not Establishment.

The only hope for conservatism, that is, for preservation of some semblance of civilized order and liberty, is a populist party along the lines of the real Reagan coalition of 1980—economic freedom and social conservatism. And the first essential objective of such a party must be to destroy and replace the Republican Party. All else is sound and fury.

I can already hear the Bush re-election bandwagon in the distance. "Get on Board! Vote Bush and Save America from Hillary Clinton!" Will the millions of our fellow citizens yet again clamber aboard and hosanna their way down the road to perdition? If so, I fear it will prove that we suffer not from bad leadership but from a fatal defect of national character.

III. THE ADVENTURES OF SHRUB (GEORGE W., 2000-2009)

FIVE MINUTES WITH GOVERNOR BUSH (CAMPAIGN 2000)

THROUGH THE GOOD OFFICES of a friend who is a large contributor to Republican causes, we were able to secure a brief exclusive interview with George W. Bush—the likely next President of the United States. We caught up with Governor Bush in Des Moines a few minutes before he was to address the annual joint convention of the Midwestern Association of Funeral Directors and the Funeral Cosmetologists of America.

Q: Governor Bush, you have promised tax cuts. Many people remember your father's famous promise of "no new taxes" and may be afraid that such promises can't or won't be kept. A related concern is that middle-and-working-class incomes are declining while the rich are getting richer.

GEORGE W. BUSH: America is the land of opportunity for everybody. We have to cut taxes to make sure people take advantage of the great entrepreneurial opportunities—like oil, and baseball, for instance.

Q: Many Americans feel deeply that abortion is a sin and a crime and that its widespread acceptance is a sign of a sick society.

BUSH: I am deeply concerned about abortion. That is why passed a parental notification law in Texas that is a model for the nation—to make sure teenagers notify their parents when they're going to have an abortion—and vice versa.

Q: Many Americans are concerned about the militarization of the federal police and incidents such as Ruby Ridge, during your father's administration, and Waco, which happened in your state. Do you think measures should be taken to identify those responsible and punish them, and to restrain such incidents in the future?

BUSH: I am the law and order candidate. As President, I will make sure the police have all the tools they need to handle dangerous criminals. When I am President, you won't have dangerous bigots like this John Rocker prowling the streets shooting off his mouth. He makes me sick. I wish we could have him at Yale for just one week, but he probably couldn't pass the entrance exam. And I want to assure my friend Charlton Heston and members of the NRA that I admire the Bill of Rights, and when I am President there will not be a lot of bad people owning guns who are not NRA members.

Q: Governor, nearly everybody realizes that public education is failing. Is it possible that the problem is too much federal intervention and that the government ought to cut back its involvement?

BUSH: I will be the Education President. I will make sure all our teachers are held to high standards and all our students have equal opportunity to the highest quality education so that they are prepared to be part of the global economy in the New World Order—which, by the way, my Dad invented.

Q: Governor, our readers feel that American military intervention in foreign situations has been too frequent and aggressive and that we ought to scale back toward a national interest policy.

BUSH: I am a conservative, a bold, compassionate conservative. America must always be ready when democracy is threatened anywhere in the world—like those people that invaded Albania. As President Kennedy said, you must bear any burden.

Q: Many people are concerned about the high levels of immigration, as well as apparently unrestricted illegal immigration, which may be drastically changing our country. Do you think one million immigrants a year is too many, not enough, or about right?

BUSH: America is a nation of immigrants. We need immigrants with their talents and skills to take advantage of those entrepreneurial opportunities that I said before. That is why I sponsored bilingual education in Texas—to help all those immigrants we need to have a strong, healthy economy.

Q: Many of our readers are concerned about what could be called judicial tyranny, that the federal courts have usurped the role of the people and lawmakers in deciding major issues. How do you feel about that?

BUSH: I am the bold conservative candidate for compassionate conservatism! I will appoint great Republican Supreme Court justices like Earl Warren, Harry Brennan, Clarence Blackmun and Ruth Bader O'Connor. And I will make sure we have diversity on the Court.

(At this point, we were interrupted by staff members reminding the governor of his next engagement.)

Q: Thank you, Governor. This has been most enlightening for our readers.

BUSH: Remember to tell them I am the conservative candidate, the true, the bold, the compassionate conservative. That's how we will win the Republican victory.

CHOOSING YOUR PRINCE

OUR FREE FEDERAL REPUBLIC, once the envy of the world, is sinking ever further into the decadence of empire. We can scarcely call "republican" a regime in which oligarchical judges contravene law, common sense, and majority will, and yet are obeyed by 270 million "citizens" with barely a murmur; in which the media of education and information contract steadily into a uniform unthinking orthodoxy of ruler worship; in which artificial aristocracies of special privilege have become steadily more entrenched.

The best evidence of the decay of the Founding Fathers' republican virtues and principles is found in our two major presidential candidates. For the first time, the American people are presented with a choice between two princes of the imperial blood. From the disappearance of the genuine aristocracy of the founding generation until today, at least one presidential candidate (and usually both) has been a self-made man—that is, someone born of humble origins who has risen to high public office by achievement or, at least, by long and prominent service to the commonwealth. Think of the origins of Truman, Eisenhower, Nixon, Johnson, Ford, Reagan, Dole, Clinton. In fact, that one could be born in a log cabin and aspire to the White House was long regarded as the benchmark of American democracy. But look at the contenders today: two preppie Ivy Leaguers born into powerful political families. Bush is the son of a president, and Gore, the son of a longtime powerful senator with insider connections to international capital.

There is little difference between them except, perhaps, that one appeals to jocks and the other to nerds.

One is a presidential candidate from Connecticut with a running mate from the District of Columbia, while the other is from the District of Columbia with a running mate from Connecticut. It seems that someone can now become president solely by virtue of being the son of a president—even a president who was rejected by the electorate. Indeed, the president voted out by the people is, along with his lackeys, set to return to power in his son's entourage.

The two pretenders, it is true, have been elected to public offices; they would not be a step from the White House if they had not been. But neither would have held any public office if he hadn't inherited his position. Both are of mediocre talent. Neither has any substantial accomplishment to his credit or any vision that could be called statesmanlike. They are celebrities, which someone once defined as people who are famous for being famous. They do not disagree more than marginally on anything that really counts; both are dedicated to cultivating the metastasizing empire at home and abroad. We are left with the right to cheer for the prince of our choice and to acclaim one (and his entourage) into power.

MIGHT HAVE BEEN

Imagining what might have been if there had been a statesman in the White House after 9/11. The President addresses the American people on September 13, 2001:

MY FELLOW AMERICANS,

As the whole world is now aware, we have suffered the most devastating attack on civilians to take place on our soil since General Sherman destroyed Atlanta and Columbia in the later stages of the War Between the States.

We will bind up the nation's wounds, and those who are responsible for this will be brought to justice, though both these things may take some time to accomplish. After every crisis in our past, America has always emerged stronger than before, and this time will be no different. In the wake of this tragedy, the American people have never been more unified. And never have we enjoyed such sympathy and good will from the rest of the world.

We must not let this opportunity pass without an appropriate response.

How did this tragedy happen? How did a handful of not-very-bright terrorists manage to strike the biggest city and the military headquarters of the mightiest nation on earth, a nation which spends three billion dollars per year on intelligence gathering? We must be honest and searching in understanding how we allowed such a catastrophe to occur, so that it can never be repeated.

The truth is that the federal government is top-heavy with too many agencies and too much personnel. We now know that information about these terrorists was available but was not noticed or responded to by the proper authorities. One alert person with the authority to act might well have intercepted them before they could carry out their atrocious deeds. I promise you that, with the best military and administrative advice available, I am going to cut and streamline our intelligence and defense bureaucracy till it is at the peak of responsibility and response. Americans have relied too much on technology and massive firepower. That is a part of our national character. But these efforts are not appropriate to the kind of warfare that we are now facing—the war of stateless, anonymous fanatics on peaceful civilians of the civilised world.

Wars are won by material resources. But victory also requires courage, incisive intelligence, and resourcefulness. These are the qualities of brave and patriotic individuals, not of collectivities, no matter how well-funded, well-organised, and well-trained. So far we have a very bad record on the kind of military action that is needed today. Our most elite forces failed to rescue the American hostages in Iran under President Carter. Our Marines were slaughtered in the Beirut barracks without even a chance to fight back, under President Reagan. Under President Clinton, in Somalia, American Rangers were killed and dragged through the streets by mobs. And now the events of September 11 during my watch. It is clear that we need a smaller, simpler, and more flexible defense.

Those who were directly responsible for these devastating attacks are dead. However, their associates, those who lead them and give them aid and comfort, the apparatus which instigated and sustained them, are yet to be dealt with. This will not call for a massive retaliation against any country, because the terrorists come from many countries. It will require, rather, elite, highly motivated units who can identify, penetrate, and understand the languages and psychology of the people they must destroy. As Commander-in-Chief, I guarantee to the American people that appropriate steps are being taken so that every criminal in any way associated with the events of September 11 will be hunted down and killed. Even should it take years and a search to the ends of the earth.

There is something else we have learned from this catastrophe. We now know that most of the perpetrators of. September 11 were in our country illegally, in one way or another. There could not be any stronger proof that our immigration laws are not being honoured. A great nation cannot, under today's conditions of terrorism, tolerate the porous borders and lax attention to immigration lawbreakers that we have heretofore allowed, under my administration and that of my predecessors. We are proud that Americans are a nation of immigrants, but we must not be a people bent upon suicide through lacking the will to do what is necessary for our safety.

We are proud also of our religious tolerance. We seek nothing but friendship and peaceful commerce with the millions of the world's peoples who follow the faith of Islam. Perhaps we have failed to be as fair and even-handed as we might have been in our role as peacekeepers and mediators in the Middle East. I pledge to the Islamic world my renewed efforts to do better in this regard. Most of the followers of Islam are good and peaceful people. But there is no question that Islam contains a tradition and a substantial element that has always preached holy war against non-believers. We will be taking definite measures to prevent, for the time being, all Muslim immigration to the United States, and to identify and deport all those now present who have in any way infringed the law. Simple prudence calls for nothing less.

My fellow Americans, let us go forward with the determination to do what we must do so that the future will find our country and its citizens safer and the world a more peaceful place. God bless you all, and God bless America.

(Instead of statesmanship George W. Bush bloviated about how the attackers hate us because we are so good, urged us to go shopping, and launched an undeclared war against a country that had nothing to do with the attacks.)

THE CEREBRAL EMPEROR

M OST OF US, when emerging from intellectual childhood into intellectual adolescence, pass through a phase of earnest search for certainty about the world. For instance, George W. Bush recently read a book (by a Mr. Sharansky, we are told) and enjoyed a revelation. He discovered, as he informed us in his Inaugural Address, that he is a Menshevik, with Zionist leanings. This is not too surprising. Verbiage about magical crusades for humanity has a powerful appeal for adolescents. The verbiage discovered by Bush Jr. is in the air we breathe and has been ever since Marx, taking his cue from the Gettysburg Address, conflated the Declaration of Independence of the free American states with the power-friendly Declaration of the Rights of Man.

Objectively considered, without superstitious awe of his office or sentimentalism about "good intentions," Bush is a liar and a criminal. Nothing surprising about that either. That is commonplace for heads of government. What is unusual in this case is that the head of government is an ignorant fool and a spoiled brat. We have entered into the stage of imperial decadence in which a clueless inheritor of the throne is a tool of his courtiers, though, like all courtiers, they must occasionally endure an outbreak of petulant self-assertion or manage a tangent of eccentricity by their lord.

The Framers and ratifiers of the federal Constitution were hardly conversant with the concept of "personality," but they were highly conversant with the histories of empires and monarchies and how rulers' defects of character had introduced distortions into the state. But about the only consideration of character that came into their view in regard to the president was that he might become too ambitious and employ his considerable powers to the detriment of the public. This was not too worrisome since it could hardly be thought that the man who would emerge from the electoral process could be other than one long and widely known for integrity, patriotism, and exceptional services to his country. The Union would not be held hostage to accidents of birth.

The Founders' assumption held true until 1836, when Martin Van Buren demonstrated that one could become president merely by being a politician, by working the system and cultivating the support of his popular predecessor. Expansion of the patronage and the electorate had brought the methods of Aaron Burr's Tammany Hall to national politics. Lincoln nailed down the point with a vengeance by becoming president with 39 percent of the vote and hardly any record of public service at all. Presidents have since occasionally been men of distinction and service, but the general trend has been downhill.

Curiously, or perhaps not, the occupant of the Executive Mansion has been ascribed more and more power and status as less and less has been required of him of character and service. The President was designed to be, as he was commonly referred to up until the War to Suppress Southern Independence, the Chief Magistrate of the Union. He was responsible for seeing that the laws were executed, appointing and overseeing those who aided him in that task, and recommending new laws as needed. He was also to be ceremonial head of state, a rather un-republican role, but one thought necessary in a world in which every foreign relation was with a state represented by a court.

In a blog discussion a while back, I was rather severely taken to task by an anonymous correspondent for slighting the accomplishments of President Reagan. For this writer Reagan represents the most valued "presidential legacy" of his lifetime. Set aside that Reagan's legacy includes a failure to deliver on every promise he made in regard to the internal affairs of the Union. Why do we need a "presidential legacy" to make us feel good? Why should a democratic people have any regard for a president's legacy other than whether or not he had faithfully executed the laws of the country? My reply was that at this time in our national life it is vitally necessary to desacralize the government by giving up the sentimentality of "presidential legacies."

How did we get to this state of emperor worship—the need to identify with "our" president, as if he were the father of our one big happy family? It would seem that for millions of Americans now, to criticize "our president" is to commit treason against what they imagine to be a family. Well, the President is not "my president." He is a rather mediocre and troublesome man who has achieved temporary (let us hope) power through a corrupt and irrational process that required of him neither an admirable character nor proven services to the country. The President is most certainly not "my commander-in-chief." He is merely during his term of office head of the Armed Forces established by law—that is, he has the responsibility for directing their operations. He is not commander-in-chief of the United States. Constitutionally considered he is not even commander-in-chief of the federal government, which was supposed to be a government of divided powers.

How did we get here? We can't blame Lincoln, who never claimed divinity. We can blame his supporters who made use of his death to erect a literally blasphemous Christ-like figure for public adoration. (Americans are completely unfamiliar with the vast literature of sacralisation that followed upon Lincoln's assassination, which was truly stomach-turningly blasphemous.) Beginning certainly with Kennedy, though with intimations at least as early as Teddy Roosevelt, the presidency was absorbed into the corrupt American culture of celebrity. The president is no longer a hero/patriot but a celebrity. When the country was under the most devastating foreign attack in its history, Commander-in-Chief Bush was performing his celebrity routine for elementary school children. The masses today would likely run screaming in fear if confronted with a real hero/patriot as a leader.

Millions of Americans are now unable to make an elementary distinction between society and government. This means that the state apparatus is no longer the servant of society, but that society is merely raw material for the emperor and his retainers.

THE MORE THINGS CHANGE

THE REPUBLICAN PRESIDENT and Party can be charged fairly with many transgressions against justice and good government:

—Waging an unnecessary war under false pretexts.

—Waging war with callousness toward civilian suffering and at great profit for favoured contractors.

—Justifying abuses of executive power by citing the supremacy of the President's "war powers" (even when war has not been declared).

—Violating due process and the traditional liberties of individual citizens, including *habeas corpus*, under plea of national danger.

—Allowing important decisions to be made by unelected officials acting in secret.

—Justifying war by invoking the unique virtue of the United States and its mission to spread goodness among mankind, with the cheerleading of self-righteous religious fanatics.

—Piling up a government debt of previously unthinkable magnitude.

—Encouraging immigration of cheap labour from impoverished foreign countries to keep wages down.

—Appointing incompetent and corrupt party hacks to important offices.

—Dictating the outcome of elections by military force and rejecting unpleasing election results in the name of upholding democracy and self-rule.

The Republican Party is guilty of all of these things—in the 1860s. Why should we be surprised that it has returned to its roots?

WHOM THE GODS WOULD DESTROY

"THE AFGHAN AIR DEFENSES still pose a threat to the United States." So Secretary of Defense Rumsfeld, the latest in a long line of robotic technocrats who have held his post (remember McNamara?), informed the world on the airways recently. If you resist Americans bombing you, then you are a threat to the United States. To resist the U.S. government is to embrace prima facie evil and to deserve destruction. Doubtless, General Sherman is smiling through the sulfur fumes. You can hear "The Battle Hymn of the Republic" in the background.

And the President himself is so incoherent that he can nasal on about enemies that are "cowardly," "faceless," and to be understood simply and only as "evil" attackers of "freedom." The first moment of clear thought tells anyone that the perpetrators were not cowardly, whatever else may be said about them. And they were not "faceless" either. They were known to the government and had been operating freely in our country. September 11 was a vicious attack on life and property. It was an attack on freedom only if we allow it to be. To misconceive your enemy is a dangerous fault.

Words are not everything, and can be used for evil (remember Clinton). However, Bush's crippled style indicates more than a problem of articulation. It indicates a lack of thought, a lack of focus, a disconnection between the words and the realities for which they are counters. And that betrays an inability to encompass the big picture, to grasp the essential elements of the situation, which is the sine qua non of good leadership and administration. Every successful statesman (and soldier) that I can think in history has been eloquent (though often laconic) in crisis, for eloquence is simply clear thought. In the President we have not a lack of articulateness, but a lack even of simple plain-speaking shrewdness.

Was ever so much deadly power at the command of one so lacking in wisdom and gravitas?

After briefing by his handlers, the President shifted from describing the situation as terrorism to describing it as "war." In law, international and domestic, "war" has a rather exact meaning. Constitutionally, that grave evocation can come only from a declaration by Congress of the existence of such a state between the United States and another state.

But the rhetorical "war" allows a shift from hunting terrorists to a war against the institutions and civil population of another state alleged to have sheltered the terrorists and one that is surely not on board the "New World Order" proclaimed by George Senior.

George Senior had the same disconnect. I recall his fuming about Panamanian rowdies harassing the wife of an American officer. There was an unacknowledged racist implication, but the disconnect was that, thanks to the federal government, such incidents occur a thousand times a day in the United States. And Senior was "sickened" by the video of Los Angeles police officers' tactics in subduing a muscular felon high on PCP. At the same time, he was authorizing the "turkey shoot" that murdered thousands of unresisting non-felonious Iraqi soldiers (not to mention the civilians).

And then, our born-again leader proclaims "Operation Infinite Justice." One would think that a Christian would understand that there is only one Source of infinite justice. But America and God are the same thing in minds like those of our leaders. We had to get rid of that slogan, not because it offends a Christian majority but because it offends Muslim sensibilities.

And while fighting a war against Muslim terrorists, we must be so obedient to ethnic sensibilities that airport security must body search little old ladies whose families have been in the country since the 1600s – to avoid "profiling." And how about the disconnect between fighting Muslim terrorists in the East while killing Christian men, women, and children in the Balkans in aid of Muslim terrorists?

A few weeks ago, our long-time member of the US House of Representatives from my district in South Carolina, Floyd Spence, passed away. He was, as politicians go, a pretty plain and honest man. He left instructions that a Confederate flag be displayed and "Dixie" be played at his funeral in the country town near which I live. However, one of the princes, Vice Emperor Cheney, refused to make his ceremonial appearance at the occasion if anything reflecting the South appeared. So, the family, the community, and the wishes of the dead must defer to the ideology of an imperial government that, with billions in treasure, cannot fend off murderous mass attacks on the population. One would think that in a crisis, some of the best American symbols of courage and loyalty would be celebrated (as they were in World War II).

Instead of correcting and punishing the incompetence and failures of the bureaucrats, Congress rises to the crisis by voting them still more billions. And our solons, in peacetime, blithely vote away personal liberties against search and seizure that are the products of a millennium of struggle, in pursuit of an illusory security.

I hope I am wrong, but so far as one can tell, the people at large have not displayed much reason or morality in their responses to the crisis. Enthusiasm to get the enemy (never mind which) resembles the fervor displayed for the favorite athletic team – a stupid but potent force. (In my area lots of people now have two flags on their vehicles – the Stars and Stripes and the banner of their favorite college team.) In decadent Rome the citizens engaged in bloody battles over the respective merits of the Blue and Green chariot racing teams with the same zeal they held against the foreign enemy.

"The increase in barbarity goes on until everything is dissolved in blind violence . . . and the pleasure of destroying and punishing," wrote Richard Weaver in contemplation of World War II. The end result, he said, is nihilism, the loss of all humane values. Long before Weaver it was common wisdom that: Whom the gods would destroy, they first make mad.

Note in passing: Americans are catastrophically ignorant of our history. Else it would be noticed that the very first war carried out by the U.S.

government was against violent Muslims. But President Jefferson did not try to convert the Barbary pirates to democracy or invite them to immigrate. He made them stop doing all the nasty things they were doing to Christians.

IMPERIAL MILITARY EXPEDITIONS

"WE Americans" (a euphemism for the ruling class) probably learned something from Vietnam. Since that disastrous war, imperial military expeditions have been conducted somewhat differently: Bomb the barbarians into submission from the air rather than try to win their hearts and minds for democracy on the ground. It may be that we haven't heard the final word on the long-term viability of this new approach, however.

As has been often said, getting into Afghanistan is easy. Getting out is the hard part. And, as far as I know, there are as yet no missiles smart enough to identify and wipe out terrorists without intelligence on the ground and subsequent mop-ups.

Secretary of Defense Donald Rumsfeld's unveiling a few weeks back of the new color-coded terrorism warning system (different intensities from yellow to red to indicate the increasing degree of threat to Americans) made me wonder how much "we" really learned from Vietnam after all. Life imitates art. Was anyone else besides me instantly reminded of the wonderful 1970s movie "Go Tell the Spartans"?

In the early days of the Vietnam War, Burt Lancaster and a small group of fighting soldiers were stuck at an isolated outpost that was governed by a color-coded panel, devised by rear-echelon whiz kids, which was supposed to show the intensity of enemy activity. Of course, it was absurd and disastrous.

The film was a perfect satire of what happens when the waging of war, an art, is controlled by robotic Detroit technocrats. Shades of Robert McNamara! Has he been reincarnated as Rumsfeld? Then we really have learned nothing. Rumsfeld has, on several other occasions, shown himself the master of gifted military thinking, as when he reported that "Afghan air defenses still pose a threat to the United States." He also told the American people, concerning Osama bin Laden: "He is either in Afghanistan, or another country, or dead."

But, alas, Rumsfeld is only a stand-in for his chief, the President, whose calls to the people in the matter of terrorism have not exactly been clarion. Eloquence is not everything, but you can hardly have true leadership in a great crisis without it. For eloquence is nothing more than clear thinking expressed in language well designed for those who need to be led. The imprecise, empty, platitudinous, trivial, ill-fitted, contradictory, and, yes, robotic, statements with which the President has declared and described both our enemies and our war might lead us to fear a lack of clear thinking at the source.

MARCHING TO PERSEPOLIS

The beginning of the words of his mouth is foolishness; and the end of his talk is mischievous madness. ---Ecclesiastes, 10:13

I DO NOT KNOW whether Chief Magistrate Bush will start an offensive war against the Persians, as is expected by many observers. I am inclined to think that even so irresponsible and morally trivial a man as Bush will draw back from the unpredictable consequences of such an action. However, I know that history is replete with catastrophes brought on by the folly of foolish and reckless rulers. I know that Bush is an arrested adolescent who has little experience in suffering the consequences of his bad actions and choices and seems unable to admit a mistake. That he has never in his life experienced the discipline in reality involved in having to do an actual honest day's work. Further, that he is catastrophically ignorant of history--the little that he knows is wrong. His view of the world is that of a corporate vice-president for public relations, and not a very good one. Also, he usually strives to please his friends among the Likudniks and the oil sheiks.

I am also perfectly certain that other parts of the ruling establishment do not have sufficient integrity and patriotism to prevent Bush from launching another war of aggression if he grabs at that option. I know with certainty that the U.S. government is in such actions in contempt of the Constitution that established it. I am fairly certain that the wars Bush has made or will make in the Mideast qualify as war crimes by the Nuremberg standard, i.e., legally they are indistinguishable from Hitler's invasion of Poland. I am convinced that Americans risking their lives in Iraq (or Iran) are badly mistaken if they think they are somehow fighting for their country.

Americans in general are giving a vivid exhibition of the folly of putting trust in Power. That they are doing so means that the wisdom of our Founding

Fathers is now forgotten, as irrelevant and alien to us as the laws of Hammurabi.

For the leaders of the people cause them to err; and they that are led of them are destroyed. --Isaiah 9:16

IN DEFENSE OF CHEAP SHOTS

SOME READERS HAVE COMPLAINED that your mild-mannered and ever temperate writer is guilty of taking "cheap shots," of making overheated accusations and using exaggerated language to describe the transgressions of George Bush and his regime. I reply that tyranny is usually incremental and always presents itself as necessary and for the public good. Thus, it should always be guarded against and opposed at the threshold. If our forefathers had not observed this rule, there would have been no American War of Independence.

George Bush wants to write his own job description without reference to law or the other branches of government. That is the very definition of dictator.

Solzhenitsyn has reminded us often that despotic regimes rest upon two pillars--violence and lies. George Bush has shown a proclivity for both.

On 9/11 we were the victim of sneaking deadly violence against the innocent. The situation called for sober, tireless pursuit of justice against the guilty (as well as correction of the government incompetence that allowed it to happen). Instead, the response was more senseless violence--George Bush inaugurated a slaughter of thousands, almost all of whom were innocent in the matter. Violence accompanied by lies. Even if the invasion of Iraq had been a success instead of the shambles that it is, it still would be an evil exercise in violence and lies. (Almost the only criticism now made of the war is that it was a blunder. Whether a blunder or not, it is still a crime.)

Various Bushites claim that the Constitution does not apply to "detainees" at the offshore jails like Guantanamo. Their purpose, of course, being to free the President's accomplices from both the due process requirements of criminal law and the civilized conventions of prisoner of war treatment. (This absurd argument is just one more of the endless consequences of Lincoln having made the government superior to the Constitution.) Any old reactionary state rights man--James Madison, for example--would have replied to Bush thus: The Constitution creates the government. The government has no existence apart from the powers granted by the people of the States in the Constitution. Therefore, nothing that the government does can be other than under the Constitution. Including the President's acts as "commander-in-chief." A President above the Constitution is a euphemism for dictator, and Our Great Decider has proclaimed that he has the right to commit our country to war at his own discretion.

The Bush government holds people in prisons offshore so that it may deprive such persons of both the protection due to prisoners of war and the procedural rights due to accused criminals. Bush contends that the offshore prisons are not subject to constitutional requirements. In this, as in so much else, we pay the price for Lincoln's having put presidential war powers above the Constitution in order to preserve his own government. I admit to being unenthusiastic about extending to foreigners the legal rights of citizens. But since the purpose of rights is to prevent officials from abusing citizens, then we should be wary of the slippery slope of allowing officials to abuse non-citizens. A more fundamental problem is that we no longer know who is a citizen and who is not since the government itself has thrown open the gates to every foreigner who can manage to get here. Much of the time, when the government makes any distinction between citizen and foreigner, it is in favor of the foreigner.

A Rubicon has been crossed. For the first time in history a President has at his own choice launched a war of foreign aggression without even a semblance of real justification. Many Germans doubtless thought that Herr Hitler was a good man looking after

his people when he rounded up dissenters and invaded Poland. After all, everyday life seemed to be going on normally and just about everybody agreed with what the government was doing. They were thinking short-term, like most Americans in response to the September 11 atrocities.

The willingness of Germans to sacrifice freedom for supposed leadership supplied by their Nazi rulers is hardly different from the servility of large numbers of Americans to absurd "security" measures after 9/11. The worst of totalitarianism, Solzhenitsyn said, was the perpetual collaboration with lies, willing or forced. When Americans, once noted for their freedom and independence, line up at the air gate to take off their shoes and throw away their toothpaste, we know there is something wrong. We are become collaborators in support of a phalanx of government lies: 1) the lie that the ritual makes us safer; 2) the lie that we are all equally suspect; 3) the lie that the government "cares" about our safety; and 4) the lie that the government knows what it is doing. And we do it without the coercion that the Soviet Union used for such exercises. Of course, the government has been for at least a half century propagating lies that we have given lip service to, but now we abet our own overt humiliation.

Some readers complained that I was too harsh a while back in discussing the late President Ford. After all, it was said, he was a nice old guy and not a bad President as recent ones go. Edward Ericson and Daniel Mahoney, in the introduction to their excellent new *Solzhenitsyn Reader*, remind us that the noble Ford referred to Solzhenitsyn, whom he refused to meet, as a "goddam horse's ass." Ford's response to one of the greatest men of our time tells us all we need to know about the worth and stature of the man. (Margaret Thatcher willingly met the Russian exile for several hours' conversation.)

Many Americans (outside of the South as long as the invasion and occupation were still remembered) have been taught that the Republican Party is the party of good and respectable people, compared with the other one. And so, it is assumed, its leaders are not bad fellows and generally do the right thing. This has seldom been true. If the good character of our country is ever to reappear, we must stop giving these dogs-in-office the courtesy they don't deserve. If it takes "cheap shots" to make an impression, then so be it.

ENORMITIES AND OTHER IRRITATIONS

PRESUMABLY LIKE EVERY LIVE BEING in the U.S. 65 or older, I recently received from the government a 152-page paperback book explaining to me the glories and the ins and outs of Medicare. Being of a perverse nature, I became interested in the numerous photographs of happy Medicare recipients and caregivers that were spread through the book to spice up the text. Of the people pictured, 23 are black, 17 are white, and 14 are Asian. There is one who might be Hispanic and one who might be a Native American. What might this statistical imbalance mean?

At Ruby Ridge, a foreign mercenary sniper in the service of the U.S. government murdered an American woman standing in the doorway of her home holding her infant. In the same military action against a homestead, her teen-aged son was also killed. No federal lackey has ever apologized or been penalized for this enormity. However, more recently, when a black teenager was killed by a citizen defending his life against a felon, the teenager in question received a vast outpouring of sympathy, including from the President of the U.S.

At Waco, the U.S. government mounted a heavy military attack (which it later repeatedly lied about) against a church, resulting in the burning to death of several dozen innocent children. No federal lackey has ever apologized or been penalized for this enormity. Instead, survivors of the attack were prosecuted as criminals. Very few Americans seem to have noticed.

Saudi Islamic terrorists hijacked planes and rendered major damage to American people and structures, including the military headquarters of the vaunted "greatest power on earth." The President, who had many connections with Saudi oil interests, made sure that his Saudi friends were whisked to safety and did all he could to minimize public backlash against Muslims. His deliberate failure to enforce immigration laws meant that the terrorists were in the country when they should not have been. His $2 billion intelligence budget failed to detect the assault, a monumental display of government incompetence. The President was re-elected and his actions received almost no criticism.

In response to the attack by Saudi terrorists, the President declared an undeclared "war against terrorism" and invaded, against international law, an unrelated country that the U.S. had previously supported with arms and money. An inconclusive invasion for which an immense debt was piled up. The invasion was justified by egregious lies of the President and his lackeys. A clearer case of treason is hard to imagine. The President was re-elected and is still venerated in some circles as a great statesman. Impeachment was never even mentioned, although the previous President had been impeached over a semantical question in regard to a sexual indiscretion that had no discernible effect on official acts.

Did any empire in history ever have such petty and poltroonish leadership as our American one? No Alexander or Napoleon, not even a Chinese Gordon--just Lindsey Graham, George Bush, Madeline Albright, and David Petraeus.

What would George Washington or Thomas Jefferson think about the Union of free men that they worked to bring into being?

The Bush Years: The Way We Are Now

OF 34 SENATORS WHO VOTED recently against English as the official U.S. language, not a single one was from the South.

Eleven Republican Senators voted to make illegal aliens eligible for Social Security, including all of those thought of a presidential material.

The IRS is now hiring private firms to collect delinquent taxes. Tax farming—one more sure sign that Empire has replaced Republic.

The White House has proudly proclaimed that the Emperor is observing the Muslim ritual of Iftar dining during holy Ramadan.

Even if someone proved conclusively that 9/11 was a Bush false flag operation, there would still be millions of people who would think that "our President" could do no wrong.

Looking at the U.S. government, maybe there is something to be said for "balkanization" after all.

Many commentators have worried that Bush's arrogant incompetence has destroyed the future election chances of the Republican party. But that is a good thing—the most positive contribution the Boy Decider could make to America would be to put a stake through the heart of the Republican party.

I am not surprised that foreign countries don't want to be bossed around by George W. Bush. I don't care for it myself and I am American.

It is reported that there are 240,000 illegal alien sex offenders at large in the U.S. Could that mean we have a dysfunctional government? In case you have forgotten, a dozen morons with plastic weapons blew up two skyscrapers and part of the command center of "the world's only remaining super power." Might there be a competence question here? The emperor is buck nekkid but nobody will say so. It would not be nice.

It is said that more than 90% of the detainees in "the War on Terror" were not captured in arms but were merely swept up on suspicion or sold to the U.S. by enterprising warlords who were rewarded out of the bottomless American treasury.

It appears that the U.S. government has more people in prison in Iraq than Saddam Hussein ever did. Maybe not treated any better?

News reporters indicate that your government has been giving "Homeland Security" grants to "American" mosques to improve their security. I feel safer just thinking about it.

For years now American society has conspired in the polite fiction that General Colin Powell is some sort of paragon of ability and integrity. I see little evidence that he is anything other than one of hundreds of similar military bureaucrats, over whom he was jumped in the service of "affirmative action." Being a good bureaucrat, Powell lied egregiously to the American people and the world to justify an illegal and unwise aggression, as ordered by his boss. In a sound country the lies, once exposed, would lead to disgrace and loss of public favour. But our Designated Hero is still presented as a great moral exemplar—because he had (in private) "doubts" about the lies he spewed forth. Rather than disgrace, we are told that Powell merits our sympathy, for our hero has suffered "embarrassment" when caught in the lie.

STATESMEN, YEOMEN, NINNIES, AND POLITICIANS

A S FAR AS THEIR PUBLIC CHARACTER as citizens goes, long observation has led me to divide people into four types.

1) STATESMEN. This tiny minority is responsible for most of the positive aspects of government. Those with original ideas and broad vision, who accomplish benevolent laws and institutions, even taking into account the welfare of posterity. Leaders who provide great moral examples by serving their people rather than themselves: George Washington, R.E. Lee, Charles de Gaulle, the late Pope John Paul II. (You can think of others. I tend particularly to admire skillful and indomitable leaders of small, beleaguered peoples, like President Kruger of the Boers and Marshall Mannerheim of Finland.)

2) YEOMEN. The ordinary, decent folk who respect the gods, obey the laws, support themselves, help their neighbours, deal honestly, and do public duties faithfully when called upon (paying taxes, defending the country, jury duty, trying to cast a responsible vote). The most numerous and indispensable class of citizens. But because they go about their own business and expect others to be as good as themselves unless proved otherwise, they tend to pay little attention to public matters, change opinion slowly, and normally trust and follow rather than, as they should, suspect and question the constituted leaders of the state.

3) NINNIES. These are people whose ideas on public questions are childish and self-centered, who desire both to conform to fashion and to be regarded as superior in daring, wisdom, and virtue to the ordinary folks. This category includes most professors, journalists, middle-level bureaucrats, political activists, and, unfortunately, a great portion of the clergy. Ninnies are responsible for a vast amount of static and pseudo-knowledge which foul communication between Statesmen and Yeomen. I suppose Ninnies can be

found in any country, but I have the impression that they are nowhere else as numerous and prominently placed as in America. (Americans began in the early 19th century to notice and decry the large number of aggressive, pseudo-intellectual, self-appointed moral superiors coming out of Boston.) Sometimes a Ninny achieves great status by serving as a front for Politicians, a classic example in recent times being George W. Bush. Ninnies are numerous on the left, but in recent years they have been found abundantly on the Republican side (example: people who think Condi Rice would be a great president). One particular right-wing subset of the Ninnies (O'Reilly, Hannity, Savage, *etc.*) displays nasty fascist tendencies.

4) POLITICIANS.   People who create nothing but control everything. Machiavelli was not only giving advice, he was describing an eternal type. Man is an institution-building animal. Statesmens' accomplishments lead to institutions, and institutions perpetuate themselves and bestow distinctions and profits. These distinctions and profits, in time, come to those who concentrate on maneuvering to position themselves well. During ordinary times of inertia and limited attentiveness, successful maneuvering for position within an institution is enough to make one seem to be important, esteemed, and useful, even if one has contributed nothing to the world or to the mission of the institution. One can achieve political power by flattering the Ninnies and seeming plausible to the inattentive Yeomen. A certain number of clever but morally defective people will early observe that the world's rewards are as often bestowed for the appearance of achievement as for achievement itself. The folk conception of a politician as one who watches which way the people are heading and then gets in front to "lead" captures this truth. It is commonplace for positions of great power and respect to be filled by people who have never in their entire lives done anything unselfish or useful for their fellow citizens or had any sincere idea or impulse directed at the public good. This category includes most congressmen, presidential advisors, bishops, media moguls, university presidents, generals, and top corporate executives. The type is universal and immemorial but, again, I suspect is particularly numerous in America, which invented the phenomenon of Celebrity—being well-known for being well-known—and where there is no measure of individual value except money. The worst part of this is that when real crises come, Politicians are in

charge and they lack the intellectual and moral resources to meet the crisis. They can only think and do what they have always thought and done— manipulate appearances to keep themselves on top. Thus Dubya Bush can never resolve the Iraq debacle because his vision of the alternatives is short-term and self-referential. He may blunder or be forced into a solution, or he may acquire a handler who can find a plausible face-saving solution, as the politician Nixon did for Vietnam.

(There is another sizable category of persons inhabiting the United States who are not really citizens at all, merely Sports Fans, Gadget-worshippers, and Shoppers.)

PHANTOM POLITICS

For the time will come when they will not endure sound doctrine; but after their own lusts they shall heap to themselves teachers, having itching ears; and they shall turn away their ears from the truth. And shall be turned into fables
—2 Timothy, 1:3-4

ILLEGAL ALIENS ARE A THREAT to your health, your safety, your life, your income, and your children's future. Your President and a majority of your Senators want millions more of them. Think about it.

Half the country hates George Bush because he is a conservative Christian from Texas. The other half likes him for the same reasons. Both groups are delusional. His title is dubious on all three descriptions. The first group (leftists) are emotionally unable to accept that he is really the best friend they ever had. The second group (Republicans) are either corrupt, too stupid to perceive reality, or emotionally unwilling to admit that they have been royally duped.

The vagueness in Bush's public persona is deliberately cultivated and very useful to an unprincipled power-seeker in gulling a public having neither common sense nor wisdom. Phantom images are a fixed feature of irresponsible power--like a "War on Drugs" or a "War on Terror," amorphous imaginings treated as if they were tangible realities. Some Romans thought Julius Caesar was a tyrant and others thought he was the saviour of the Republic. Actually, he was simply a gifted power-seeker.

Marketing of fantasies is a long-standing feature of American public discourse--pioneered by Republicans: American System; Slave Power and Free Soil; Rum, Romanism, and Rebellion; Saving the Union (a union cannot be saved by force--it becomes something else). The Democrats updated and perfected it (until Bush surpassed all previous performances) with Making the

World Safe for Democracy, a Nation of Immigrants, the New Frontier, the Great Society, etc.

I never cease to be surprised at the short-sightedness of the news media and American public in regard to public affairs. It is as if there is no past, only a present publicity image. Everyone expresses shock that George Bush turned out not to be a "conservative." From the time he was governor of Texas it was already blaringly obvious that he was a big spender, an advocate of open borders and federal takeover of education, a man who would say anything to get elected and who purged principled conservatives in favour of mediocre toadies and amoral manipulators.

Yet I continue to hear people who say they were deceived when they voted for Bush in 2000. (Some of them even voted for him a second time.) The main deception going on was self-deception. The same swindle is being repeated with Romney and the same patsies are falling for it.

Many Americans are dumb enough to believe that they are "defending their country" by attacking a foreign people that have done them no harm and pose them no threat. Defending one's country has been turned into a phantom unanchored in reality.

The grasping at phantoms can be seen in media explanations of the Virginia Tech murders committed by an Asian immigrant: "crisis of young males in a feminized society"; "an oppressive environment causing students to break down." As soon as the first word came out the media and officialdom switched into a compassionate and maternal pose. I kept trying to find out the actual facts of what happened and who the killer was amidst endless stories about the sadness of survivors. The second day I still had no facts. There was an orgy of juvenile self-pity and wishful thinking and no hint of an adult desire to recognize facts, much less deal with them. The media told me that the "tragedy unfolds." It was if some mysterious plague had descended.

My local carpetbag media aided evasion of reality by going berserk over an incident that occurred at the same time: a 12-year-old girl brought a knife to school. As if there was some connection. There was, of course, not the slightest relevance except in the minds of those who imagine "student violence" as some disembodied problem hovering in the atmosphere over us all. The only explanation that had any substance was given by alternative media: "immigrant mass murder syndrome."

Another phantom: "9/11 changed life in America forever." More and more our "news" resembles this. It is not a report of what someone did or something that happened. It is not even an opinion; it is a "feeling." The "news" has abolished all distinction between fact, feeling, and entertainment. Many Americans apparently suffer from the delusion that making war in the Mideast somehow protects them, when the opposite is fact. Politics has disappeared. There is no contest over interests, policies, and principles. There is only a huge amorphous audience emoting together and following their own benevolent and all-knowing leader.

We live in a society that is driven half-mad by phantoms that have supplanted common sense.

THE PRESIDENTIAL PRESS CONFERENCE
THAT WILL NEVER HAPPEN (2007)

Q. MR. PRESIDENT. Justin Raimondo, antiwar.com. We just passed the sixth anniversary of 9/11, and Osama bin Laden is still at large and more influential than ever, while hatred of America seems to be growing in the Mideast and other parts of the world. Is it possible the U.S. has been following the wrong strategy in the War on Terror?

BUSH: They hate our freedom you know. As President Kennedy said, you must sacrifice any burden. That great American thinker Nathan Whathizname said that too. I read the book.

Q. Mr. President. Stephen Heiner, Fleming Foundation, a follow-up, please. But the 9/11 I terrorists were already over here--most of them illegally. Doesn't that suggest the need for better immigration control?

BUSH: I am proposing a new comprehensive program of immigration reform that will solve the problem of amnesty once and for all.

Q. Mr. President, Chilton Williamson, *Chronicles*. Figures released recently indicate that in the last two years over a thousand Americans, including more than 50 police officers, have been killed by illegal aliens from Mexico . . . .

BUSH: Anti-Americans prevented my comprehensive plan for immigration reform--which we will accomplish next year despite anything those un-American bigots and haters may say. . . . America is a land of immigrants and all faiths are welcome here. Mexico enriches our country with its wonderful hard-working people and family values and lawn care and Islam is a religion of peace. Look at great Mexican-Americans like Alberto Gonzales and Mel Martinez--and, uh, Sammy Sosa.

Q. Mr. President, Wayne Allensworth, *Russia Report*. Some experts feel that the U.S. is following a policy of deliberate hostility toward Russia, when we ought to be pursuing a path of cooperation. Some believe that Mr. Putin, for instance, is actually cleaning up some of the previous corruption.

BUSH: As Condi will tell you, Russian policies are beginning to threaten world stability, like undermining democracy where we have some of our bases in Asia.

Q. Mr. President, Paul Craig Roberts, columnist. Many people think that our present trade policies are increasing the gap between rich and poor, undermining the middle class, and making America into a Third World economy. What is your opinion on that belief?

BUSH: My administration has created almost a million jobs which shows you that NAFTA is working for McDonald's and other companies. America is the land of opportunity--this is why the terrists hate us for our freedom and we must not cut and run from the War on Terror. And I ask all Americans not listen to gloom and doom and keep on shopping.

Q. Mr. President William Lind, Free Congress Foundation. Some economists and observers have expressed great concern that so much of our national debt is owned by China, that this puts our economy in a very vulnerable position . . . .

BUSH: They are willing to give us their money. That just shows you how they admire us for our freedom and democracy and how great free trade is when my Dad was Ambassador over there for democracy. I hope we can soon say the same great thing about Mexico.

Q. Helen Thomas: Mr. President, it has been reported that you recently acquired a big ranch in Paraguay. Can you tell us why and if you are making plans for your retirement?

BUSH: They have some very interesting animals there that we could use in Texas. Besides, Dick said it was a good idea. No more questions. I have a meeting with President Umgum-uh, that fellow from Upper Volta where I decided to do more to help them having more AIDS.

MORE THOUGHTS ON THE WAY WE ARE NOW

Alas! it is delusion all;
  The future cheats us from afar,
Nor can we be what we recall,
  Nor dare we think on what we are.
—Lord Byron

S UPPOSE THE U.S. were to suffer a major economic catastrophe, leaving millions in distress. Which of the two scenarios below more closely reflects what will happen:

A. Congress meets and in grave deliberation seeks wisdom and understanding of how the catastrophe happened, how it may be remedied and prevented in the future, and how the people may best be helped.

B. Congress meets. The members make haste to look after their own interests. Then they take care of those who have influence over them or who they need to stay in power. Parties blame each other for the catastrophe. Congress finally responds to public demand by enacting a complex, plausible-sounding short-term remedy, although nobody knows whether it will really do any good or not.

*   *   *

Suppose the following events: Mexican thugs cross the border and attempt to take over a ranch in Arizona. In the process they wound the rancher's eight-year-old daughter. The rancher and his son return fire and in the ensuing firefight two Mexicans are killed. One of them, it is later contended, was only 15 years old and had no weapon. The thugs retreat to the Rio Grande, pursued by county sheriff's deputies. Mexican police officers fire from across the river to cover the escape of the thugs. One deputy is wounded.

Which best describes the likely response of President Bush:

A. Bush demands that Mexico apologize, punish the offending police officers, and deliver the attackers to the U.S. for trial. He honors the ranch family and the wounded deputy in a White House ceremony.

B. Bush apologizes for the loss of Mexican life, denounces vigilantism, and pushes prosecution of the rancher for murder and violation of civil rights.

* * *

A lot of folks took delight when Dan Rather was caught reporting a false story about George Bush's National Guard record and had to retire. I have always been glad to see folks like Rather and that other TV truth-seeker Sam Donaldson succeed. They exemplify the greatness of America as the land of opportunity. They prove that in America you can be ugly, dim-witted, and completely lacking in personal appeal—and still become famous and a millionaire!

* * *

How far Americans have advanced toward the status of contented imperial subjects is indicated by the silly and false assumptions that are taken for granted by millions:

"The President is our commander-in-chief." The President was never intended to be the commander-in-chief of the country, or even of the federal government. He is commander-in-chief of the armed forces. And the armed forces only operate according to laws and regulations made by the Congress and under appropriations that expire every two years. The President was made commander-in-chief to ensure civilian control of the military, not to establish presidential control of the citizens.

"Let the courts decide." It is hard to imagine any more abject surrender of a people's right of self-government. This is the plausible seeming excuse of legislators who, out of cowardice and expedient self-protection, have allowed the federal courts to foist one social revolution after another on citizens who never consented to them; in fact who never even had the opportunity to vote them up or down.

"The two-party system helps democracy to work." In fact, no device was ever invented more effective in making sure that democracy does not work than the two-party system. Its purpose and function is to guarantee that no real challenges are ever offered to the rulers.

"The Republican Party is the party of conservatism and free enterprise." In fact, the Republican Party has never, ever opposed any government interference in the free market except those that might benefit labor or harm Big Business. The Republican Party is and always has been the party of state capitalism, whatever its deluded voters might think. In its rise to power it was revolutionary, destroying the political heritage that went before in order to establish the power of state capitalism. By state capitalism is meant highly concentrated private ownership and wealth with government protection and subsidy.

"Enemy combatants." A term used by the Bush government to describe people it holds in prisons offshore so that it may deprive such persons of both the protection due to prisoners of war and the procedural rights due to accused criminals. Bush contends that the offshore prisons are not subject to constitutional requirements. James Madison would have a simple answer: The government is a government of limited and specific powers which are delegated by the people of the States. The government does not exist except by virtue of the Constitution. Therefore, there can be no activities of the government that are not under the Constitution, wherever they may be.

A MUSLIM AMERICA

EMPIRES, WHICH ABSORB peoples of varied traditions, have a tendency towards religious syncretism. Differing beliefs are considered equal and are tolerated as long as they do not come into conflict with the worship of the supreme state. This seems to have been the case with religion under the Roman and Japanese emperors. In such a situation traditional faiths become optional and even interchangeable, while the power of the state grows and it becomes more and more the center of devotion and veneration.

There is no reason to think that our current American Empire is immune to these tendencies. Indeed, there are many signs to confirm that we are headed in that direction. President George W. Bush has again and again in public statements, far beyond what mere polite inclusiveness requires, insisted that all religions are equally American. He has gone out of his way to welcome adherents of the major Asiatic religions, and has relentlessly affirmed the compatibility of Islam with the American way. Islam has now been observed in the White House and incorporated into the previous American formula of "Protestant, Catholic, and Jew." Some polls indicate that Americans' opinion of Muslims actually became more favourable after the September 11 attacks.

Christianity is pre-eminently an anti-imperial religion. Its predominant stance has always been for a separation of power between secular and religious authority. "Render unto Caesar . . ." Among all faiths it is the most oriented toward a relationship between the individual person and his Maker, makes less of worship as a group or societal obligation. Further, Christianity rests upon a balance of reason and imagination, full employment of both sides of the human brain. It flourishes best in a culture that is led by mature, well-integrated personalities such as were predominant in the American past.

Immigration has already given the United States the multiple faiths of an empire, not even considering the far-flung projections of state power across the world. The simple affirmation that America is a Christian (or indeed a Western) society is increasingly denied in the highest circles. Islam is increasing its power in the United States—not only from immigration but from conversion of natives and immigrants of other faiths. (Its increasing recruitment of Hispanics has been observed.)

Perhaps equally relevant is that the level of intelligence in the United States has been going down, at least since the 1960s. This is bound to increase the strength of Islam, which is preeminently the faith of the slow-witted and literal-minded. Its appeal, which should not be under-estimated, is in its simplicity. It claims to be universal and requires belief in a simple dogma. Islam provides a veneer of dignity and order for primitive people--an increasing portion of the American population.

George Bush has stated repeatedly that all faiths worship the same God, i.e., they are identical. He is not a Christian at all but a Unitarian/Universalist--an emperor for all tastes. His theology, and that of many of our countrymen, is identical with his politics--a conflation of God and America. Americanism claims to be universal and it requires only a belief in a simple dogma--global democracy. And it increasingly venerates the Presidency as the supreme source of light and truth.

One of the tenets of the Americanist faith is that all traditional faiths are subordinate to and equally respected by the Empire. Bush has proudly announced that the Muslim rite of Iftar is observed at the "American" White House, presumably along with the usual "Christian" prayer breakfasts. While Bush holds out his arms to Islam his supporters beat the drum for war against "Islamofascism." Is this not a contradiction? Not really, for imperialists naturally try to subsume the enthusiasm of both sides in a conflict between subject peoples. Not that George Bush is intelligent enough to understand or plan this. He is merely following the path of immediate expediency and of least resistance. Since their religion is Americanism and not Christianity, it would not be surprising if the Republicanised political preachers of the "Religious Right" segue into the universal imperial religion. They are, after all, theologically ignorant, poltroonish opportunists, and lickspittles of power.

Islam may well turn out to be the convenient faith for such a society as the United States is becoming. It is the most compatible of the major faiths with empire. Indeed, George Bush seems already to think of himself less as a constitutional official than as the occupant of the supreme Caliphate. One can even imagine, without too much of a stretch, a post-Presidential Bush ensconced in the palatial fortress of the Green Zone in Baghdad as the new leader of the imperial religion.

CAMPAIGN 2008

I ADMIT TO EXTREME ANNOYANCE at people who voted for George Bush the first time (and even twice) because, they claim, they were fooled into thinking he was a "conservative." The only fooling going on was unforgivable self-delusion. George Bush had not a single conservative in his entourage or among his friends, advisors, or mentors. He had purged all conservatives from the Texas Republican Party and replaced them with his personal apparatchiks. He was a notorious friend of illegal aliens and as Governor had pushed through a law giving illegals free access to state colleges. A major plank of his platform was federal takeover of public schools and the federal invasion of religion by grants. He prevented Pat Buchanan from speaking at HIS convention. All of this was glaringly and painfully obvious in 2000.

Of course, you will say that in a presidential "debate" Bush advocated a "humble foreign policy." When did something a Bush says in a campaign have any relation to what he does in office? Bush's leftward drift, takeover by the Neocons, and huge expansion of federal power and expenditure would have happened even without 9/11. There was no great change or conversion after 9/11—only an acceleration on the path he was already on. To move toward a leftist concentration of federal power is the attractive path of least resistance for any administration.

I am further continually astounded by the apparently widespread hallucination that the Republican Party is the "conservative" party. In its entire history of a century and a half the Republican Party has never conserved anything. It has never had as a goal the intention of conserving anything worthwhile. It has instigated revolution in the service of certain monied interests and has acquiesced in every radical change as long as those interests were not threatened.

It is now a commonplace to say of our past eight years that "conservatism" has been discredited forever by George W. Bush and his followers. Conservatism has not been discredited but Republicanism has. However, leftists much prefer to announce the death of conservatism, a possible obstacle to their agenda, and keep around Republicanism--one of their many assets.

What a degraded public life we enjoy. Surely there must be in this broad and fair land, unknown to fame, several million men and women more qualified to be President than Obama, who is no more than a media-hyped celebrity. Or for that matter, more qualified than George W. Bush or "Mitt" Romney.

GOODBYE, GEORGE

An American president can wreck his country and blow up the world, but he cannot recreate either of them. —Chilton Williamson

A RECENT BOOK on the George W. Bush presidency is called *A Tragic Legacy*. But tragedy suggests the fall of something high and noble. There never has been anything high and noble about Bush. His career began as low comedy and ends as bloody farce.

How many killings does it take to make a war criminal? Is ignorance and incompetence a defense?

Nothing is so easy and gratifying as spending other people's money---especially if you are praised for your good works--- and get a cut yourself. This is the long-established cynical practice of Congress. But with Bush one has the sense that it is something else. In his own universe, which he mistakes for the world, he has no experience with the consequences of over-spending and debt. Consequences of any kind have little reality for him. Moral responsibility is not part of his universe.

Shopping is the great American pastime. Everyone likes to participate whether they are good at it or not. One of the high points of George's reign was when, just after catastrophic terror attacks, he urged his fellow countrymen to comfort themselves by shopping.

Or perhaps the highest point came when it was pointed out that Al Quaeda was not a problem in Iraq until after his invasion. Showing the pungent truthfulness and courageous spirit of the true patriot and statesman, Bush responded: "So what?"

Can you imagine a post-emperor Bush? Here is a man who has never done anything worthwhile, who has never done a single thing to serve his fellow man before or during his public career. What is such a man to do now?

If Americans learn nothing else from the Bush fiasco, assuming they are able to learn anything, it should be never again to elect a spoiled brat to high office.

Perhaps George's most lasting "accomplishment" is the discrediting of Christianity as a political force in America. It is assumed that his strongest support came from "evangelicals," with whom he pretended kinship. Liberal commentators like to imagine that Christians conspire to impose a puritan reign of terror on the country, and so pundits and historians will continue to write about the evil domination of the Bush administrations by Christians. But of course, this is to misstate the facts, as usual.

The fact is that the Republican party has always dictated to the organised "evangelicals" but they have never dictated any Republican act or policy of significance. In the 1960s George Wallace showed the vote-getting potential of the "social issues," something which no Republican had the insight or daring to do. But the party did see the potential votes from "silent majority" rhetoric. And so the "leaders" of the organised "evangelicals" were seduced by pretenses of fellowship and shared values. For the most part, those "leaders" were people of such shallow intellect and character that once allowed to actually meet a President they were enslaved for life. They wanted more than anything what too many Americans want—superior respectability and status within the herd. (Both Tocqueville and Solzhenytsin observed that this is a predominant aspect of American behaviour.)

But, of course, the Republican politicians generally hold in contempt the Christian groups and their concerns, a minor distraction from their pursuit of power and profit. They have had zero impact upon Republicans in power. The last believing and practicing Christian in the White House was Jimmy Carter.

Given the disgrace brought down on the faith by Bush, there will probably never be another.

HOLLYWOOD DOES BUSH THE LESSER

I FORCED MYSELF recently to watch Oliver Stone's movie takedown of George W. Bush called "W." I have a morbid curiosity about cataloging trends among the pseudo-intelligentsia. This film, like previous productions of the same auteur, is doubtless providing multiple thrills for the type in America and Europe.

As readers here are well aware, I hold no brief for Bush Minor, a morally and intellectually defective man who has done irreparable damage to our country. If anything, the film, while exposing his defects clearly, is actually too sympathetic. Bush is portrayed as an almost tragic figure. But his career is not a tragedy; it is a nasty farce. One gets the impression, no doubt intended, that George W. was inevitably doomed by being a Texan, a born-again Christian, and from an ambitious family. This message is re-enforced by the background country music.

Of course, there are the natural limitations of the docudrama, essentially a form of fraud which makes up acts and words from imagination and applies them to real events. The purpose is usually propaganda rather than history. (Of course, some of our most celebrated historians these days do the same thing.). Josh Brolin gives a tour de force acting job as W., but it does not work. He is better looking and more masculine than George Bush and he lacks that slight hint of squeeze-faced, sneering New England ninniness that dominates Bush's face. ("What, me worry?") Brolin's screen accent is more Southern than Bush's, doubtless to make the point about the evil brought about by Texanness.

The portrayals of Cheney and Rumsfeld don't convince me—neither Richard Dreyfuss nor Scott Glenn show enough arrogance and force. Colin Powell, as played by Jeffrey Wright, is not very convincing in addition to being portrayed as more noble and independent-minded than the real thing. Barbara Bush is played by Ellen Burstyn as feisty, but she misses the supercilious, contemptuous Yankee flavour of Babs' demeanour. Thandie Newton does a great job of presenting the insipidness of Condi Rice, however. I am undecided about James Cromwell's portrayal of Bush Major—perhaps because one has less sense of his private person than the others.

My favourite moment is when candidate Bush avows he will read the whole Constitution and even learn parts of it if necessary. Reminded me of freshman history students, most of whom have never read the Constitution and can make no intellectual connection with it if they do.

There are, of course, some things that one won't get from this highly doctored account of history. For instance, some words never appear in the two hours: Israel, neoconservatives, Douglas Feith, Office of Special Plans, Project for the New American Century.

IV. DEFRAUDING DIXIE: SOUTHERN REPUBLICANS

J. STROM THURMOND, R.I.P.

J STROM THURMOND DIED ON JUNE 27, 2003, answering that last great Roll Call in the Sky at the age of 100, shortly after finishing out a half century in the U.S. Senate. He won his first election before Bill Clinton and Junior Bush were born. He spent the last period of his life near his native place, the Black Belt town of Edgefield, South Carolina. (Can anyone imagine Bob Dole going back to Kansas or the Kennedys to Brookline?)

Thurmond's life, rendered as a novel, would be classed as a fantasy. There is little point in discussing his politics, which illustrate nothing except the revolution of federal expansion that has taken place since the 1960s. He is better understood as a life force, a museum-quality specimen of evolutionary adaptability.

Aside from the third of the population made up of recently arrived Mexicans and Rust Belt refugees, there is no one in South Carolina who did not know Strom personally. (I met him, through no effort of my own, two weeks after arriving in the state in 1971.) He was known by his Christian name "Strom" as readily and familiarly as anybody in these parts since Elvis. There was a genuine feeling of loss at his passing, though it was long anticipated. He out-lived several groomed successors. Thurmond was liked by the people not because he was a "conservative," although he vaguely symbolized the visceral conservatism of the population. Not only did everybody know him, there were few constituents who had not received from him personal assistance in some encounter with the many-headed federal beast.

Edgefield was long the fire-eating heart of Dixie, the home of Preston Brooks who thrashed Senator Sumner of Massachusetts with a cane. (The cowardly Sumner had used his office to vilely slander good people, but refused to accept a challenge.) Also the home of "Pitchfork Ben" Tillman, who threatened to do something similar to Grover Cleveland.

A graduate of Clemson College back when the all-male students were still uniformed "cadets," Thurmond began in local politics. During World War II, he resigned a judgeship to join the service. (At the same time, Richard Nixon and Lyndon Johnson were maneuvering to get out of the service and into office.) At the age of 41, he rode a glider into Normandy on D-Day and returned with numerous decorations. Thurmond belonged to those several generations of Southerners who considered the Armed Forces to be the heart of manhood and patriotism. Like most such, he continued to be a strong supporter of "defense" spending long after the forces had ceased to embody either of those qualities.

A popular and dynamic veteran, Thurmond was elected governor in 1946. He was soon thrust—or thrust himself—onto the national scene. Southerners came back from the war flush with patriotism and barely aware of the fact that they were being set up as the next official enemy of the United States. They soon learned, however, as the Democratic Party began to reject its traditional Southern base and pass into control of urban minority groups and Jacobins. (The Republican Party, always 50 years behind on the leftward trajectory, is presently attempting the same maneuver.)

Out of the postwar revolution in the name of "Civil Rights" came the States' Rights Democratic Party of 1948, with Governor Thurmond as its presidential candidate. He carried four states and over a million votes—more than the liberals' darling Henry Wallace—and gathered a small but significant following beyond the Potomac, including Robert Lee Frost and the young Murray Rothbard. It was trivial remarks about this campaign that gave the Bush administration the excuse to get rid of the unlamented Trent Lott as Senate leader.

Illustrating Americans' terminal ignorance of history, the media obits made much of the point that Thurmond was once a segregationist and an opponent of "civil rights" but had undergone a reformation. It sounds as though segregation were some inexplicable personal shortcoming rather than the law and the overwhelming preference of millions of white Southerners (and of most Northerners in practice, if not in theory). A survivor like Thurmond will naturally adapt to changed circumstances. From the early 1970s on, his appointment of black staffers and outreach to black constituents involved no change that was not the common experience of the South. The change reflected two things: (1) inevitable submission to the federal juggernaut and (2) white Southerners' good manners and basic good will toward black Southerners. Like most of us, Thurmond accepted in personal good faith the conditions that Northerners had imposed out of abstract righteousness and absentee moralism. (Massachusetts, New York, and Illinois are still the most segregated states.)

In 1954 Thurmond was elected to the Senate as a write-in candidate, the only such in American history. In the 1960s he garnered more national attention as a feisty opponent of the radical legislation of the day. He broke the record for filibusters—forty-eight hours holding the floor—and challenged his opponents to an arm wrestling contest. There were no takers, if I remember correctly. He got further attention by a timely switch from the Democrats to the Republicans during the Goldwater episode.

The Great Society changed American government forever, making the feds the fount of all blessings in nearly every realm of life. Thurmond and other Southerners who wanted to stay in power joined the new regime which transformed members of Congress from representatives of the people to middlemen for the government's payoffs to the people. If Northern Republicans and Democrats insisted on voting vast spending programs, then a rational Southern response was to get a good place at the trough and pipe as many goodies as possible back to the homefolks.

Strom's patronage machine worked so well that it kept running long after he had slipped into dozing senility. This is not to be despised considering the country-club cookie-cutter Republicans who have succeeded him. Nor was it without some positive benefits---federal judges in these regions are not generally the crazed gauleiters that flourish elsewhere in the country. Strom was one of the few Southerners to use the Republicans more than they used him.

Thurmond to a legendary degree, suffered from the politicians' common malady of testicular hyper-activity. Reported early exploits make Bill Clinton look like an amateur. At 49 he married a young beauty queen and at 69 a 22-year-old coed. In later years his affinity for the fairer sex took on a slightly comic courtliness. My most vivid memory of him comes from the Clarence Thomas hearings. When Strom addressed some of the witnesses as "ladies" he was taken to task by a feminist virago, doubtless from Massachusetts. The last soiled tatters of Western civilization in America versus a triumphant New World Order.

DÉJÀ VU (2006)

TWENTY-THREE REPUBLICAN SENATORS joined a large majority of Democrats to vote for the Bush bill to amnesty millions of present and future illegal aliens. The bill passed the Senate 62–36.

The Republican Senators supporting amnesty and future immigration increases were from Maine (2), New Hampshire, Rhode Island, Pennsylvania, Ohio (2), Kentucky, Indiana, Minnesota, Kansas, Nebraska, Utah, Idaho, New Mexico, Arizona, Oregon, Alaska (2), Virginia (Warner, military-industrial complex), South Carolina (Graham, presidential hopeful), Tennessee (Frist, presidential hopeful), Florida (Martinez, self-explanatory).

Thirty-six Senators voted against electing a new American population in place of the present one. Four of these were Democrats from West Virginia, Michigan, Nebraska, and North Dakota. The thirty-two Republicans Senators who went on record against the President's atrocity against our country were from Virginia, North Carolina (2), South Carolina, Georgia (2), Alabama (2), Mississippi (2), Tennessee, Kentucky, Louisiana, Texas (2), Oklahoma (2), Missouri (2), Arizona, Nevada, Wyoming (2), Montana, Utah, Colorado, Kansas, North Dakota, South Dakota, Iowa, Pennsylvania, and New Hampshire.

The South was the only part of the country to give a majority vote to the patriotic side, though with considerable help from the Plains and Rocky Mountains. The regional vote was similar in the notorious Immigration Bill of 1965 which is responsible for our present troubles. The South was the only part of the country to vote a majority against that bill of forty years ago. There is one change between 1965 and 2006. The Southern patriotic vote is less strong because establishment Republicans have made inroads into some States and there are more leftist Democrats from gerrymandered affirmative action districts as a result of the executive and judicial interpretations of the Voting

Rights Act of 1965 (which a majority of Republicans voted for, twice). In 1965 there were still a lot of genuine Southern Democrats around to vote against traitorous legislation.

If you want to run up the figures you will find the same pattern of regional voting on gun control, abortion, balanced budget and equal rights amendments, and many other matters—Northern, Midwestern and West Coast Republicans supporting the left-wing positions and the South providing the most substantial opposition.

Are you surprised that a number of Southerners decided several years ago that the Union was irredeemable and the best we could hope for was to save our own part?

DÉJÀ VU AGAIN (2006)

"It's amazing what you see when you look."
—*Yogi Berra*

ON SEVERAL OCCASIONS, without eliciting much response, I have pointed out the pervasive hold that the Northeast, especially the corrupt extremist States of Massachusetts and Connecticut, has on presidential and vice-presidential nominations. Especially the Republicans, but also the Democrats except when they win elections with candidates from the South.

Why the Republicans continue to be in bondage to the Northeast is a serious mystery and, I believe, a key to understanding the situation of the United States today. Republican strength today is in the Heartland and South. Massachusetts and Connecticut have few Republicans and almost no real Republicans, but the pattern of their dominance continues. We are told that among the front runners for the nomination to succeed the present Connecticut president are the leftist Mayor of New York City (next to Connecticut) and the Governor of Massachusetts, a Mormon who nobody had ever heard of until recently. Where did that come from? And George W. Bush is supporting the leftist Democratic Senator and Vice-Presidential candidate from his native Connecticut instead of the genuine Republican nominee.

I am taking bets that neither Guiliani nor Romney has a chance of being nominated as far as the voters are concerned. However, both stand a good chance of being chosen by the Powers That Be for a vice-presidential nomination once the troublesome grassroots has been neutralized.

Previously I pointed out that the Senate vote on the recent Bush administration "immigration reform" bill (to replace the American people with Third World coolie labour) showed a division that was more regional than party related. The South and the Mountain West were the only regions that voted against the treasonous bill. Republicans from the Northeast, Midwest, and Pacific voted overwhelmingly with limousine liberal Democrats. The regional pattern of support and opposition to immigration resembled the pattern of the 1965 Immigration Act, when most Southern Democrats voted against the bill and most Northeastern and Midwest Republicans voted for it.

The treason legislation passed the Senate 62 to 36. Here is an interesting (at least to me) breakdown of the vote.

New England:
11 traitors (4 Reps., 6 Dems., 1 Independent)
1 patriot (Rep.)

Mid-Atlantic:
9 traitors (8 Dems., 1 Rep.)
1 patriot (Rep.)

Industrial Midwest:
9 traitors (3 Reps., 6 Dems.)
1 patriot (a Democrat)

Agricultural Midwest:
7 traitors (4 Dems., 3 Reps.)
5 patriots (3 Reps. and 2 Dems.)

Pacific:
10 traitors (7 Dems. and 3 Reps.)

The Confederacy:
8 traitors (4 Reps., 4 Dems.)
14 Patriots (14 Reps.)

(The Republican traitors from the South include several with national aspirations. They are in a long line of Southern mountebanks who foolishly have dreamed of national office. In their entire history the Republicans have never nominated a Southerner for President or Vice-President. They never will.

The Republican Party came into existence for the purpose of exploiting and dominating the South. That remains one of the chief points in its agenda. The two Democrats from Arkansas, a corrupt borough owned by the Wal-Mart and Tyson coolie labour giants, hardly count.)

Border South:
6 patriots (5 Reps., 1 Dem.)
1 traitor (a Republican)
1 Dem. Not voting

Mountain West:
8 patriots (Reps.)
7 traitors (4 Reps. and 3 Dems.)
1 Dem. Not voting

Clearly, the South and the Mountain West are the only regions left where the Old America is robust enough to contend for dominance. And the South and Mountain West already have been and are being adulterated by immigrants from the Third World and the Northeast. (On net, the Republicanisation of the South may well be a setback for conservatism.) The homogenization of regions into the Northern pattern proceeds apace, progressively eliminating any possible social and cultural base for conservatism. The Powers That Be like it that way, agreeing with Karl Marx that "a people separated from their history are easily persuaded." We can hope that, as time moves on, conservatism will enjoy an American revival, but don't hold your breath. Have a nice day, and remember to press 1 for English.

WEEP FOR CAROLINA

BY NOW EVERYONE WHO CARES (and many who don't) knows about the collision between the honourable Ron Paul and the vulgar demagogue Giuliani at the Republican presidential candidates 2007 "debate" in South Carolina. (These events are not really debates at all but more like joint press conferences.) Mr. Paul raised the question of whether Americans might be targets for terrorists in part because of actions of the U.S. government. The grandstanding New Yorker demanded a retraction and apology. How could anyone be allowed to doubt that everything the U.S. government has done has always been noble and good? How could anyone think that foreigners could ever have cause to hate us except for perverse resentment of our very goodness?

When the South Carolina audience applauded Giuliani's tantrum I was not surprised at all, but felt a sting of shame. How far Calhoun's "gallant little State" has fallen. There is no excuse for my State, but I can perhaps offer some explanation in expiation.

Remember that since 1965 our elections have been controlled by commissars from the U.S. Justice Department — an oppression carried by the votes (several times repeated) of "conservative" Republicans. One of the highest comedic points of 20th century American politics came in the mid-sixties when the windbag Republican leader, Senator Dirksen of Illinois, announced his support for the second Reconstruction of the South. It seems that during a lonely midnight stroll in the deserted Capitol, the ghost of Abraham Lincoln appeared to the Senator and instructed him how to vote.

A great deal of national force has been exerted in the last half century to make Dixie give up its peculiarities and join the American mainstream. It seems to have worked only too well.

Then too, our State has been the final destination of many, many people from elsewhere. In fact, we seem to have replaced Florida as the favourite resting place for well-heeled persons from colder climes. Half our people, nearly, are from out-of-state — which means that even a higher percentage of Republicans are and a yet higher percentage of the Republican donors likely to be invited to such events. Many of our new citizens are fine folks, but it is a sad fact that the Democrats, white and black, are more native-born than the Republicans. I have always tended to agree with Burt Reynolds in one of his movies when he remarks of the local crime boss that he was a murderer, a thief, and a pervert, but worst of all he was from out-of-state.

Further in our defense, I might point out that Southerners came out of Reconstruction as the stepchildren and whipping boys of a corrupt and cynical national politics. The only way to get ahead was to beat the crooks at their own game — ergo, Lyndon Johnson and Bill Clinton. And thus the most important cause of the present degradation of South Carolina: the evil legacy of Strom Thurmond. Thurmond's masterpiece of a self-centered career left us with the simple visceral reflex that politics consists entirely of two things: booty and patriotism, the latter being defined by support for the military. Unlike John C. Calhoun, no present-day South Carolina politician would ever leave the side with the patronage to dispense merely on a matter of principle or policy.

Grandmother, who was always right, said you should always have something good to say about people, even if you could not avoid calling attention to their shortcomings. To their credit, I think my Carolinians are motivated by a basically healthy instinct of loyalty. Some bad guys hurt us on 9/11. Honour requires that we hurt them back. Under such circumstances, it is bad form to criticize the home team, especially if there is a losing season because the coach is something of a dunce.

We should never underestimate the power of inertia and cultural lag in public life. Most folks had their formative political experiences in the Vietnam era when opposition to the war usually looked like disloyalty in word and deed. (The real reasons for opposing the war made little impact on the people at large at the time.) The trouble with such virtue, of course, is that unguided by intelligence it can attach itself to very unworthy objects. To sum up, my people, alas, suffer from the same maladies that are epidemic among Americans in general — shallow and myopic perspective due to the scarcity of intelligent, honest, and far-sighted leadership.

IT'S TRUE WHAT THEY SAY ABOUT DIXIE
(2010)

THROUGHOUT MOST OF AMERICAN HISTORY region has been a better predictor of political position than party. That aspect of our reality has been neglected and suppressed in recent times as the rest of the country has conspired or acquiesced in transforming the South into a replica of Ohio.

Yet the notorious squeak vote on the Obamacare bill shows that the old reality still exists and that the South is still the core and mainstay of any viable American conservatism. My late friend Bill Cawthon ran down the statistics on the House of Representatives vote. Of the four census regions, the South was the only one to vote against the federal takeover of medicine. The South (the Confederacy plus Kentucky and Oklahoma) voted 71 per cent against the bill; the Northeast 75 per cent in favour; the West 61 per cent aye; and the Midwest divided evenly.

Every Southern State voted a majority negative. The no vote included 19 Democrats from the South. If you remove the four sparsely populated Plains States of the western Midwest, the Midwest total moves to a majority in favour of Obamacare, even allowing for the no-vote of the Southern Border State Missouri.

This pattern has held on every major piece of legislation since 1965, even allowing that Southern Congressional districts are designed by federal lawyers and judges to maximise the minority vote. Immigration, balanced budget, public prayer, women in combat—the South has provided the brake on the leftist agenda of federal grasp. Of the 212 nay votes on Obamacare nearly half (100) came from the South.

A century and a half ago, John C. Calhoun, one of the most prescient observers of the American regime, remarked that the South was the balance wheel of the Union which prevented the whole from flying apart under the stress of the manias that regularly seized hold of the mainstream. It looks as though that is still true, though our ability to control the machine grows weaker year by year.

HOPE DYING

(As I feared in this little commentary in 2010, Haley has since gone full Republican.)

O UR SMALL BUT PROUD STATE can't seem to stay out of the political spotlight. We had barely recovered from the exposure of our present Governor's exotic extra-marital affair when we made the headlines again as a result of the surprising outcome of the Republican primary for the next governor.

As you have probably heard by now, State Representative Nikki Haley (nee` Nimrata Randhawa) took 49 per cent of the vote, swamping three well-known Republican aspirants. The Establishment Republicans and Neocons, who are always interfering and positioning themselves, seem to be claiming Mrs. Haley as their own. Very possibly she will be co-opted by them, *a la* Sarah Palin, but the outcome of the election was not a victory but rather a serious defeat for the Republican establishment. To this point, Mrs. Haley's showing looks more like a Tea Party type rebellion than the emergence of one more Republican celebrity. Her biggest campaign theme was anti-tax.

She has rendered two Establishment Republicans into has-been, also-ran nobodies: the present lieutenant governor, a rich carpetbagger doofus in the mould of George W. Bush and the darling of the press, and the present attorney-general, a reliable party man endorsed by Rudy Guiliani. The run-off election on June 22 will be between Mrs. Haley and the next highest scorer, U.S. Representative Gresham Barrett. Barrett is as honest and as conservative as one can be and still be a Republican. The outcome will be interesting and not necessarily easy to assess.

Mrs. Haley was born in South Carolina to Sikh parents, immigrants from India. Her father practiced medicine in an impoverished rural area. Her siblings have succeeded in legitimate businesses and a brother is a career Army officer. She married a local man who is prominent in the National Guard, attends the Methodist Church, and has participated in the usual public service activities. She has served responsibly as one of the members of the lower house of the General Assembly from my populous suburban county. She has, as far as I know, never played the race card. Indeed, the black vote is negligible in our county and in Republican primaries, although the carpetbagger vote is large.

Being a fan of the British Empire, I have a soft spot for Sikhs, who were a creditable part of the British Army for so long. In Texas it used to be said that a nasty mob required one Ranger to deal with it. It was said in the Raj that one Sikh could deal with a nasty mob of Muslims or Hindus. Please, Lord, if we must be flooded with immigrants from India, and we must whether we will or no, let them be Sikhs and not Muslims and Hindus.

The shifting demographics of our State (even more evident in our esteemed neighbour to the north) render the election results something of a puzzle. In the 1964 election Hubert Humphrey got only 30 per cent of the vote in North and South Carolina. In 2008 Obama got 50.3 per cent in North Carolina and 45 per cent in South Carolina. We are obviously witnessing here a large demographic transformation. This has nothing to do with the black vote because the black percentage of the population has been diminishing in both States with the influx of white carpetbaggers. It is estimated that half our Republican voters were born elsewhere. Our coasts and mountains are dotted with gated communities full of mini-mansions inhabited part of the year by rich Northerners. Our cities are filled with lower-middle-class refugees from the Rust Belt seeking subsistence employment where the economy has been until recently still growing.

Further, thanks to the feds, the Chamber of Commerce, and that heroic and far-seeing statesman George W. Bush, our Mexican population will before long be 10 percent, and Asians, black Africans, and West Indians are numerous enough to be noticeable in any public place.

Our State is still very conservative by American standards. Three hundred years of brave and independent spirit do not disappear over-night. But that conservatism should not be conflated with the Republican Party, which here, as always and everywhere since the days of Lincoln, has been an electioneering machine whose aspirants will say anything and do anything to get hold of the power and perks, and whose only real agenda is maximising the use of the government to increase their wealth.

For South Carolina, which long prided itself on never knuckling under to either party, this is largely the heritage of Strom Thurmond, who easily morphed from Dixiecrat rebel into the earth's biggest and longest-lasting patronage artist. Remember, we are the State that produced the evil, principleless election manipulator Lee Atwater, godfather to Karl Rove.

Shortly before the election, two Republican hacks, connected to the lieutenant governor, held a press conference to announce that they had both had illicit affairs with "that woman," Mrs. Haley. It was implausible, to say the least, when the two pathetic operatives were viewed in relation to Mrs. Haley, a quite handsome woman. The public showed good judgment and her poll numbers shot up. We South Carolinians seem to have had more than our fair share of rakes in office, but it is well to remember that always and everywhere "politician" is a synonym for "rake." We may even have elected one or two closeted types, if rumour is to be credited, but at least we have never elected a flagrant faggott. Unlike certain Deep North States that politeness forbids me to mention, although one of them starts with "M" and ends in "s."

CAROLINA, I HARDLY KNOW YOU

IN THE PRIMARY OF JUNE 10, 2014, the Republican voters of South Carolina gave a comfortable victory to Lindsay Graham, one of the most notorious and repulsive of the current "invade the world, invite the world" brand of U.S. Senators. Friends from elsewhere have questioned me repeatedly: how could this happen in such a traditionally conservative state? One recently wrote: "What the heck happened down there? How did the war-monger, open-borders, amnesty-crat Miss Lindsay win the primary?" Indeed, it is a legitimate question. How can this armchair warrior be the choice of a state that once produced Francis Marion, Wade Hampton, and the Strom Thurmond who rode a glider into Normandy on D-Day and married a beauty queen forty years his junior?

The short answer is that, politically, South Carolina is no longer a Southern state. It is something exactly opposite—a Republican state. Much misunderstanding arises from the long-lived and widespread delusion that a Republican state is the same thing as a conservative state—that the dominance of a Republican party machine is somehow a guarantee of political conservatism. This delusion is and always has been so patently at war with reality that those who suffer from it must be considered defective in intelligence or lacking in sincerity.

Of course, incumbency and money usually tell in any election. I received in the mail every other day for two weeks before the election a slick multicolor mail-out praising the great conservative Graham. Had he not notoriously stood up to Obama on several occasions (although never on anything important)? Does he not support war and "defense" spending to the limit? What else could you want for "conservative" credentials? One of these mail-outs was designed to facilitate absentee ballots—doubtless for the use of our numerous affluent carpetbag voters who spend the warm winter with us and retreat to cool New Jersey in the torrid summer. And the bachelor Graham proved his family values by portraying himself with his sister and her offspring. It required extraordinary effort even to learn the names of his opponents. Most of the voters never knew these names until they saw them on the ballot.

It has not yet fully penetrated public consciousness that, of our State's population, half were not born here. That is the white people. The African American population is more native-born but is also receiving foreign increments. The Carolinas are now serving the role that used to be played by Florida—the preferred destination of refugee Northerners. Some of those newcomers are very fine people who joined us for the right reasons. But most are simply ordinary Americans (whether upper, middle, working class, or military retirees) of the kind who are clueless enough to vote for Mitt Romney or Lindsay Graham.

A Carolina accent can scarcely be heard in the cities now. You have to go to small towns and the country to talk native. The speech of a cultured Carolina lady, the most beautiful sound on the North American continent, is giving way in the younger to Valley Girl. It is sad to see something you love being swallowed up in cultural mediocrity. (I am not even counting change brought by the Asians and Mexicans who are numerous enough to be conspicuous.)

North Carolina, having been a target longer, is in even worse shape. The state that not very long ago elected and re-elected Sam Ervin and Jesse Helms failed by only a fraction in giving its vote to Obama in 2008 and did so in 2012.

But this is not the full explanation. To understand you have to know that the Republican party is and always has been primarily an election machine. It is a vehicle by which the ambitious—either stupid rich men or the upwardly mobile devoid of all ideas and principles—seek a rise to power. Its greatest asset has always been a vague appeal to respectability. A great many Americans long for nothing more than the status of respectability, to feel superior to the "Rum, Romanism, and Rebellion," that was successfully attached to the Democrats for so long.

The Republican machine has money and skillful operatives. It learned to appeal to the Wallace voters and thus vault Reagan into the Executive Mansion. But even before this happened the machine had forced Reagan to accept one of its own as running mate. Of course, the Wallace voters received nothing in return from the administration, but they have remained useful as a bloc of voters by default. A bit later, many people were encouraged by the political organization of religious conservatives, which it was hoped would bring some morality back into public life. But the leaders, longing for respectability, were easily co-opted by the Republican machine. The religious conservatives never received anything except lip service, but they remain a reservoir of default voters.

There is no reason to doubt that the same thing will happen to the upstart "Tea Party" movement. Indeed, its co-option is already underway. Lindsay Graham had one promising opponent, articulate and principled state senator Lee Bright. Bright was endorsed by the Tea Party. But the Tea Party also endorsed three other candidates, none of whom got out of single-digit support, and thus hopelessly divided and confused the anti-Graham vote. Having had in my misspent youth some experience of the work of Republican operatives who posed as friends in order to throw monkey wrenches into principled movements, I cannot help but suspect the same at work here.

NONE DARE CALL IT TREASON:
THE AMNESTY VOTE (2013)

I T IS NOT A STRETCH, perhaps, to regard the Senate vote of over two-thirds (68-32) in favour of mass amnesty for illegal aliens as signaling the eclipse of the historic American people, those brave and liberty-loving folk who created the United States out of a continental wilderness. The bill has the Orwellian title 'Border Security, Economic Opportunity, and Immigration Modernization.' A good many of the senators who voted for the bill were around to vote for earlier immigration laws that they knew would never be enforced.

Much less attention is paid to the political differences of regions these days than used to be the case, except for occasional references to Red and Blue States or when occasion arises to exorcise the South for being the center of all evil opposition to the progressive agenda. But region remains a major consideration to the extent that traditional roots and attitudes persist in some places.

My fellow secessionist, the late Bill Cawthon, paid attention to those things, and his analysis of the Senate vote on amnesty showed the same thing that he found to be the case on every leftist measure passed in the last half century or more. The South is the only region that has voted a majority against revolutionary measures.

In the entire northeastern United States (24 votes) only one senator voted nay. The vote of the Pacific States was unanimous for amnesty, including all Republicans. From the industrial Midwest (10 votes), hardest hit by deindustrialization and unemployment, only three senators voted against. Obviously the ruling class of this region dances to the tune of limousine liberal global democracy rather than tend to the dreary business of looking after the plain folks.

The agricultural (Trans-Mississippi) Midwest did somewhat better with half of 14 senators voting nay on amnesty, although one Republican joined the treason contingent. The senators from the Mountain States voted 11-5 for amnesty. Four Republicans from this region voted yea.

Amnesty support was solid for Colorado, New Mexico, Arizona, Nevada, and Montana, and four Republicans from this region voted yea. Only Wyoming and Idaho were solid against.

Overall, 14 Republicans voted with the Democrats to "legalise" the aliens.

Only the South had a majority against amnesty, 16-10. There is little comfort in this figure, however, because the Southern vote against previous amnesties was bigger and even included some Democrats. There are now more leftist Democratic senators from the South than ever before---all six voted for amnesty. More significantly, *four establishment Republicans from the South voted for amnesty.* These, of course, included the repulsive Lindsey Graham. Interestingly, Miss Lindsey's appointed African-American colleague from South Carolina, Tim Scott, voted with the patriots against amnesty.

As might be expected, Virginia, Florida, and Tennessee are lost to the South. The bulk of the Southern nays came from Border and Deep South States that have been least affected by immigration, North Carolina, which not too long ago elected and re-elected Sam Ervin and Jesse Helms, gave Obama a near-majority in 2008 and a majority in 2012. The State has been a dumping ground for masses of Mexicans and Asians and of Northerners feasting on the relative prosperity. The Carolinas have now replaced Florida as the favoured location for affluent Northeasterners fleeing the mess they have made in their home States. (I know of a gated island near Charleston with 200 secluded semi-mansions. It is virtually empty in the summer, but in the winter rife with New Jersey license plates.)

A curious exception seems to be Texas. Despite the vast Mexican population, both senators voted against amnesty. It would seem that Texas is assimilating Mexicans rather than *vice versa.* That may be because Texans have a real Southern culture to assimilate to, while elsewhere the new immigrants merely join in the existing nonculture.

A FATAL BLOW

ALAS, TEA PARTIERS, you may as well fold your tents and quietly leave the field. "Salon" (a website that apparently caters to members and would-be members of the national elite) has given your movement the coup de grace. They have uncovered the cruel truth that your movement is a "Southern" movement. No more need be said. The taint is ineradicable.

According to "Salon," 67 per cent of the supporters of the movement come from the South. They also hint darkly that the teenage level percentages of "Tea Party" support that come from the Midwest and West are probably people cursed with Southern blood in their family tree. This is probably true. It is also likely that some of the adherents in the South are Rust Belt refugees.

For readers of "Salon," the fact itself is decisive and conclusive. Whatever comes from the South, in this case populist resentment of the federal government, is beyond redemption by being identified as Southern. They can count on a good part of the public to react on cue with the same automatic hostility and disdain.

What "Salon" reports neither surprises nor frightens folks down this way. Every populist movement in American history has come from the South. There is no other kind. In America, anti-government populist movements are always conservative—they look back to a past better time and they have a Jeffersonian suspicion of government. The South is the only part of the country that has a historical memory that goes back more than a week and that still contains something of original American feeling.

However, Salonites need not worry. People's movements in this country are invariably taken over by slick operators from above the Potomac and Ohio who turn them into commercial ventures. (This happened to the campaign that grew around Judge Roy Moore of Alabama for his stand against federal obliteration of the Ten Commandments.)

Speaking of numbers, it is reported that after the recent carnival in the federal city, the public approval of Congress has fallen from 27% to 14%. The only thing curious about this is—Who are those 14%? My guess is people who keep sports channels turned on all the time. The number of people who are intelligent enough to know that party conflicts are meaningless for the fate of our country are too few to show up in the numbers.

SENATOR NO: HOW A SOUTHERN CONSERVATIVE BECAME A NATIONAL REPUBLICAN

Show me a hero and I will write you a tragedy.
—F. Scott Fitzgerald

Review: *Here's Where I Stand: A Memoir* by Jesse Helms

IN HISTORICAL TERMS it was not too long ago, a half-century or less, that old-line Southern Democrats, with their seniority and solidarity in Congress and maverick governors like George Wallace were a significant force in American politics. Jesse Helms went to Washington the first time (1950-1953) as a staffer for one of those, Senator Willis Smith. Helms's autobiography covers that, as well as his small-town Depression-era origins, his career as a broadcast executive and editorialist that made him a candidate for the U.S. Senate as a newly minted Republican, and his 30 years in the Senate (1972-2002), including his chairmanship of the Foreign Relations Committee.

Jesse Helms is a unique, and probably unrepeatable, phenomenon. He was five times elected U.S. senator from a State that is larger than is commonly recognized, despite a well-deserved reputation for refusing to play by many of the normal rules of politics and a professional and political background different from most senators. He won five statewide elections against opponents with potfuls of out-of-state money and the opposition of every daily newspaper in the state. After and before each election, the press announced that his victory had been a fluke and could not be repeated.

This autobiography displays many of the characteristics that one likes to think belong to the man himself. It is candid (in an extroverted sense), humorous, charitable to opponents, and firm in avowing the continued correctness of positions taken. You can see here the feisty but good-humored, above-board, and likable personality that was at least partly responsible for his political success and that went a long way, as he became better known in Washington, toward softening the hostile impression of "Senator No."

Despite a reputation for intransigence, Helms as senator clearly understood the difference between compromising on the possible and abandoning principle. There is no pomposity, self-absorption, or convenient obfuscation in his recollections. He tells on himself the story of one of his assistants, visiting in the bowels of the State Department, seeing a framed picture of the senator in a place of honour. Expressing some surprise at this, Helms's man was told that the portrait was a reminder that "the enemy is always watching."

Future students of later 20th-century politics will have, in this work, a useful and different perspective to consider about a good many things of importance. While Helms does not deal in gossip and personalities, his recollections do give interesting glimpses of the presidents and other greats and near-greats on the national scene during his time. To give a few hints only: Nixon did, indeed, lie to a friendly freshman senator about Watergate. From retirement, Sam Ervin telephoned his successor almost daily with advice. There are many more such nuggets. Helms's experience as a reporter and editorialist, I daresay, makes him a livelier storyteller than most politicians.

Helms clearly regards his chairmanship of the Senate Foreign Relations Committee as the most important aspect of his career. He believes he was instrumental not only in thwarting many bad appointments and projects, but in reversing a virtual monopoly on foreign policy by the State Department bureaucracy, and returning decisive control to the president and Congress. He has not retreated in the least from the stand that it was right to support bad governments when they were barriers against the far greater evil of Communist expansion. At any rate, Helms's account of how he navigated the Senate and dealt with the State Department will be of continued interest to those who study such things in the future.

I said that Helms's autobiography is candid-at an extroverted level. Yet there is a deep contradiction. In his comments on recent times, Helms has never met a Republican president or Republican policy that he does not like. He avows satisfaction at the triumph of conservative forces in American politics. At the same time he admits failure in the causes that brought him to prominence: abortion, school prayer, busing, affirmative action, arts funding. To close out his career as a complete party man is a strange, though probably inevitable, climax to the national career of one who rose to notice and power as a lonely die-hard for principle.

The chairman of the Republican National Committee was reported recently as apologizing for his party's "southern strategy," though doubtless he does not intend to give back the 7 out of 10 national elections that the strategy helped to win. Jesse Helms's career was part and parcel of the forces that made that strategy successful. His five-minute television editorials after the news, which went out across vast rural, conservative regions of North Carolina on the Tobacco Network, were an eloquent expression of the white South's response to the ferment of the civil rights era. I know. I was there. I heard them. You would never know that from the autobiography of the senator who now thinks federal appropriations to fight AIDS in Africa is a high priority.

The important story in Helms's career is one he never acknowledges and perhaps, does not even recognize. It is the taming and mainstreaming of Southern politics by co-option into the Republican party.

V. THE STUPID PARTY AFTER BUSH: OBAMA LITE

THE UNNATURAL ARISTOCRACY

A LITTLE REMEMBERED PROVISION of the U.S. Constitution: "No title of nobility shall be granted by the United States" (Article I, Section 9). By this proviso the Founding Fathers affirmed the republican principle that nobody is entitled to power merely because of who he is. Americans wanted to repudiate the hereditary privilege of the Old World by which people had power in government by virtue of birth, often without merit or usefulness to the commonwealth. Thomas Jefferson and John Adams agreed that republican government should be in the hands of a "natural aristocracy" of talent and virtue. Jefferson said that no one is born with the right to ride with boot and spurs over the backs of the citizens. Adams feared that the people might be misled by the glamor of high birth into choosing the wrong rulers.

If Americans took this provision of the Constitution seriously, Barack Obama would never have been allowed to run for president. All of his adult life Obama has been treated as a privileged aristocrat because of who he is. He came to every position he has filled without any record of legislative, administrative, or military service or accomplishment. He has been raised to power entirely because of his birth. There are tens of thousands like him spread throughout all the ruling institutions of the United States. He has a smooth manner and a gift for low-key demagoguery, but no other qualifications for the most powerful office in the world.

An unnoticed irony is that this first "African American" president is not really an "African American" in the usual sense of a descendant of American slaves. He is an African, son of an African petty chieftain, from a family who were very likely slave traders, and of a crazed white Midwestern 60s radical of an all too common type. Anyone who wants to understand the Obama lineage should read the works of the forgotten outstanding writer Robert Ruark on Kenya: *Uhuru!* and *Something of Value.*

Obama profited from the widespread disgust and demoralization created by eight years of George W. Bush's ignorance, incompetence, deceitfulness, and unrepentant fecklessness. He also profited by the accident of not being of full-blooded African descent. Although they will never admit it, American egalitarians have always secretly preferred mixed bloods to full-blooded Africans. All you have to do is remember the number of almost-white slaves who appear in *Uncle Tom's Cabin*.

Some people seem to be upset that Obama has been showing signs of the behavior of a Third World dictator. Why should this be any surprise? That is what most of the people who voted for him and celebrated his rise to power wanted him to be. If that is really the case, the only remedy is an opposition party—one that is articulate and determined and can appeal to the people with courage and honesty about the sad state of the Union. But there is no opposition party. There is a self-serving, principleless organization called the Republican Party. It has not been an opposition party since at least the 1930s. It is merely a device maintained by the ruling elite to absorb and neuter discontent—a somewhat prettified carbon copy of the dominant party.

THE WAY WE ARE NOW (2008)

T HIS YEAR it is more important than ever to rally 'round the Grand Old Party and save the country from those Democratic liberals! We just can't let them take over!

Just imagine, if the Democrats get in we will have a huge national debt, undeclared and foolish wars, affirmative action shoved down our throats, federal take-over of education and everything else in sight, rampant abortion, "gay rights," open borders, government giveaways to foreign countries. We will even have more terrible Supreme Court justices like Warren, Brennan, Blackmun, Stevens, Kennedy, and Souter!

Seriously, sad as it is to contemplate, it is only too true that Obama and McCain do each appeal to large segments of American society as it is today.

However, it makes little difference who is on the throne. Junior Bush has established that a President can do anything that he wishes, at home and abroad, even in peacetime. Bush has lied to the people and Congress, blatantly usurped power, shredded the last rags and tatters of the Constitution, committed the country to an illegal and stupid war, and failed to guard against real enemies. The President cannot be effectively stopped by Congress or the people, even when he is, like Bush, of weak character and intellect and manipulated by unelected courtiers. He has suffered no punishment except low poll numbers. The U.S. in all but name meets the formal definition of a tyranny.

Where such power exists, it will always be used. There is no rewind back over the Rubicon.

Since all candidates belong to the same ruler class, it only matters to them and their retainers which one sits on the throne. The personality of a particular emperor might make an insignificant, temporary difference. A contest between the military-industrial wing of the ruler class and the candidate of the affirmative-action wing amounts to little, especially when both are merely creatures of the media wing.

What a tremendous waste of time, energy, and hopes in caring which will sit on the throne, in evaluating the words of candidates when their words are silly semantic games that would embarrass a high school debate team and will cease to have any significance as soon as the polls open on election day.

This election will be just one more meaningless popularity contest between the dumb jocks and the clueless nerds, just like the last five presidential non elections. Since the jocks have won the last two, the nerds will probably be allowed to win this one, especially since their candidate, though a nerd, is an exotic one.

Looks like I am writing in Calhoun again this time. Not that it matters.

WHY SAVE THE STUPID PARTY?

SINCE THE 2012 ELECTION there has been much discussion of the future of the Republican party. Can it ever again win a national election, or is it doomed to permanent minority status? The most common response has been that the party must "reach out" (i.e., compete in the offer of bribes) to the exploding Hispanic population. Rather neatly and deceitfully avoiding the obvious fact that Republican sponsorship of mass immigration is the cause of their minority status.

A few fringe commentators have urged that the party instead do more for its core constituency of conservative white people. But the party leadership has already repudiated this alternative in both word and deed. They have apologized for "the Southern strategy" (though not for the numerous elections that it won for them). The alternative strategy would not be respectable, and no people are more terrified of being thought unrespectable than the Republican leadership. The world view of the Sixties revolutionaries is now the mainstream, and to challenge it identifies one at once as a clueless or malevolent occupant of the disreputable fringe.

Conspicuously absent from this discussion is any explanation of why the Republican party should continue to survive at all, must less flourish. Why should we care?

It is easy to understand why people vote for Obama. He represents his constituents. He speaks for them. He promises them ever more goodies. He satisfies the ideological malice of leftists and gratifies the resentment of minorities against old America. If you are a bailed-out banker, a defense contractor, an employer of immigrant labor, or a politician eager for the perks of office, you might be tempted to vote Republican. But why bother? Being a Democrat would serve you just as well. There is no valid reason for anybody else to vote Republican.

True, there has been a kind of assumption for half a century now that the Republicans represent a conservative bulwark against leftist revolution. But is this true? Has it ever been the case? This impression is partly due to historical accident. The Republican leadership are elitists with no interest in "the social issues." But in the 1960s George Wallace demonstrated that there were votes to be had there, and so the party leaders grudgingly began to give lip service to them. They never had any intention of doing anything in regard to abortion, school prayer, affirmative action, the growth of federal power, or any other non-economic issue.

There is an impression that the Republican party is "pro-business" or pro free enterprise. Well, yes, if your business is big enough to buy government favors. What has the party ever done for the other businesses that make up the bulk of American enterprise?

The Supreme Court nominees who were supposed to turn the court back to a more restrained role have betrayed that promise again and again. And again. And again.

The Republican party does not represent its voters (and never has). It represents only itself. Consider: the strength of the party is now in the Southern, Plains, and Rocky Mountain states. The presidential and vice-presidential candidates (Romney and Ryan) were both from the deepest and most liberal North. Republican voters are conservative Christians. Neither candidate could be said to represent that viewpoint. Republican voters are much concerned about the effects of recent immigration policy. Neither candidate had any sympathy for that position—quite the contrary. Republican voters are concerned about the loss of manufacturing jobs and the ongoing proletarianisation of the middle class. Both candidates are on record with contradictory policies.

Republican voters are opposed to Obamacare, perhaps the single policy inclination most widely shared among them. But the head of the Republican ticket is the inventor of Obamacare. Republican voters were clearly disturbed by the trillion-dollar bailout of misbehaving bankers. No help there. While

Republican voters are rather too inclined toward jingoistic responses to foreign threats, it cannot really be said that they want to start unnecessary wars, support a worldwide military empire, or watch Americans being killed abroad and pay for the privilege. Yet Romney was the most imperialist candidate in recent times.

The Republican nominations were not made in a political convention. There was no political convention. It was an infomercial. The only candidate with any principles and ideas, and who had aroused any grassroots enthusiasm, was completely shut out.

Note that the appeals for the survival of the Republican party never say why that is a good thing or what positive results might be expected from that survival. They simply assume that is something that is unquestionably desirable. The simple truth is that the Republican party survives only by the tactical employment of the great state-sponsored wealth of people who want to keep it as it is and by election laws which have made it nearly impossible to change the duopoly that controls American political action. Both parties curry favor with the media and allow them unchallenged control of political debate. A situation which obviously violate the rules of democracy and the spirit of the Constitution.

But the Republican offense is more than just a failure to represent its voters. It has actively swindled them. Every groundswell of movement against business-as-usual politics that has appeared in the last half century has been co-opted, absorbed, and destroyed by the Republican leadership.

Insanity has been defined as doing the same thing over and over and expecting a different result. Those who have continued to vote Republican are perhaps not insane, but they have certainly exhibited irrational behavior and an inability to think outside the box that has been made to confine them.

BRING ON THE GOP!

THE AWFUL OBAMA is pushing terrible things on our country like socialised medicine, big spending, corporate bailouts, affirmative action, and amnesty for illegal aliens. He must be defeated so the Republicans can get in and push socialised medicine, big spending, corporate bailouts, affirmative action, and amnesty for illegal aliens.

Obama is conducting two endless and pointless wars in Asia. He must be stopped so that the Republicans can get in and start another endless and pointless war in Asia.

Obama is making terrible appointments to the Supreme Court. He must be defeated so the Republicans can get in and appoint great conservative jurists like Earl Warren, William J. Brennan, Warren Burger, Harry Blackmun, John Paul Stevens, David Souter, and Sandra Day O'Connor.

The Democratic leadership is protecting crooks and perverts in Congress. The Republicans must get a majority so they can protect their crooks and perverts.

The Republican Party has completely failed as an opposition party. It is their turn to get in power so they can be the majority and the Democrats can be a real opposition party.

Obama is too liberal. We must replace him with a conservative Republican like Mitch Romney, Michael Bloomberg, John McCain, Jeb Bush, or Newt Gingrich. (Forget Lindsey Graham and Mike Huckabee because whatever their ambitions, the Republican party never has and never will nominate a Southerner for President; or even for Vice-President.)

What the Republican Congress Will Not Do

TREAT THEIR ELECTION victory and new majorities as a mandate for anything other than enjoying additional power and perks and maneuvering for the White House in the next election.

Repeal Obamacare.

Block the Obama illegal immigrant invasion. They may adopt some cosmetic "compromise" invented by PR men which will pretend to be both compassionate and firm, i.e., "moderate."

Secure the southern border.

Replace Boehner and McConnell with leadership with some guts and principles.

Stop useless, dangerous, and counter-productive meddling in Eastern Europe, the Muslim world, and everywhere else.

Repudiate their neocon Trotskyite foreign policy.

Reign in the federal judges who are dictating "same-sex marriage" to the States.

Cut spending.

Eliminate any of the Great Society and subsequent institutions that are using taxpayer money to destroy traditional society.

Block any appointments of left-wing extremists to judgeships that Obama may make in his remaining time.

Propose anything containing a genuine idea or principle rather than an advertising slogan.

Get rid of affirmative action.

Address the immense fraud in Medicare and Medicaid.

Do anything substantive towards retiring the catastrophic national debt or eliminating dependence on foreign bond-holders.

Reduce taxes on the middle and working classes.

Save Social Security.

Put unemployment among Americans over profitable employment of foreigners.

Confirm really good men and women to the federal bench.

Pass anything containing an authentic substantive reform instead of a public relations gimmick.

Do anything to stop the ongoing proletarianisation of the American middle class.

It Won't Be Long Now (2014)

There was some things which he stretched, but mainly he told the truth.
—Mark Twain

THOSE WHO ARE STILL ADDICTED to the useless and indeed pernicious vice of following U.S. politics—let me urge you to go into recovery now. The habit of abstinence must be well-established soon or you will be tempted by the hoopla of the 2016 Presidential sweepstakes. The primaries are only two years away and the uproar will start long before that. Without a determined recovery you will have to endure an endless carnival of water temperature testing, trial balloon floating, absurd and short-lived ambitions and enthusiasms, and arrant speculation. It will all be pointless and ephemeral and have absolutely no relevance to any genuine process for selecting the next "Leader of the Free World" and Great Decider.

There is no hope that any statesmanship or even real leadership can emerge from the carnival. The American political system, and alas probably also the American people, left behind any such possibility long ago. What we will see is a contest of superficial celebrity backed by special-interest pandering that can have no meaning for any serious lover of his country. In case you haven't noticed, the U.S. is now a glorified banana republic culturally and politically, if not quite yet economically and militarily.

Nobody can predict the future, least of all a mere historian. There are often long-term changes under way that nobody notices until they suddenly emerge. And the course of our poor human race through time takes place in the mind of God, Who may disregard the plans and expectations of men. Allowing for such, we can make some projections based upon recent history. I will venture a few predictions. Anybody who likes can remember and call me to account at a later time.

The Democratic presidential nomination will be contested between the minorities, who want to maintain their prominence, and party regulars who want a practical chance to push their agenda, though of course the true nature of the struggle will not be admitted. How this will turn out is unpredictable. The ideal candidate, who can hope to capture the Obama enthusiasm, will be a minority woman with Establishment credentials. Let's keep in mind always that no matter who is the candidate, the leadership of both parties is owned body and soul by the financiers and the neo-conservatives.

The Republican nomination will be hotly contested because it will be expected that it is the GOP's turn for the top spot, especially since the Obama bubble has burst for many people. The Republican money men and the professional politicians who serve them while serving themselves almost always pick the candidate. Whether you know it or not, that is exactly what we mean when we say "the party of Lincoln." If a maverick somehow gets the nomination, he will either be torpedoed like Goldwater or co-opted like Reagan. So we can expect to see a field of Romney-like wannabes, the usual photogenic and respectable Deep North corporate types, which could include a carpetbag governor of Florida. It will be mildly amusing.

It is true that there is considerable unrest, unfocused and futile, at the Republic grassroots, and that the old appeal of the lesser evil is getting somewhat threadbare. But doubtless there are still plenty of Republicans out there who still have not figured out that by voting for the lesser evil they are accomplices in turning their country over to evil. And sometimes it is not even the lesser. And there are still the sad types who prattle about restoring a Constitution that ceased to exist long ago.

A maverick candidate, who is wise, brave, and somehow able to communicate with the people over massive jamming by the media, could perhaps get a message across about the real dangers to the commonwealth (debt, imperial over-extension, the ongoing proletarianisation of the middle class, to mention just a few). We can be certain that the two parties will never touch a real issue, which might upset their cozy relations with each other and the media. For such an outsider to succeed would require extraordinary circumstances indeed. However, he might accomplish the wrecking of the Republican party, which would be a great service to the restoration of good government.

Then again, we may not even have to go through the process at all. Obama may well succeed himself. All it would take is for the Supreme Court to declare that the two-term limitation in the Constitution violates the 14th Amendment and is invalid. This would be no greater usurpation of power than the black-robed deities have already exercised more times than can be counted. Who will say them nay? Certainly not the shallow and cowardly leaders of the Republican party. They will make a deal for themselves, the people be damned.

DON'T LOOK ANY FURTHER, MR. REPUBLICAN HAS BEEN FOUND! (2015)

R EPUBLICANS HAVE NOT BEEN TOO HAPPY lately looking over the long row of their Presidential wannabes. It is almost embarrassing— so many outstanding candidates. They all have much to be said for them, but each one seems to have something lacking, to be just not quite right. They are just not "Presidential" enough. But relax Republicans, your ideal candidate has been found at last. He is so perfect he might have been designed by computer. (Maybe he was.) This candidate fits every requirement for the ideal Presidential Republican candidate.

What do I mean? First, the ideal Republican must have the appearance and the intellect of a dreamboat senior class president. He should look like an American, someone you would be happy to have for a next door neighbor. Not a trace of "ethnic" although his love for all races, creeds, and colors and readiness to support them must be unquestionably stalwart. He must be from north of the Ohio River.

The ideal candidate should not have any experience in foreign affairs. He will naturally be a man of the finest good ole American common sense, always choose what is right and just. He will know he will have to rely on the wisdom of the neocons, now well-established masters of Republican foreign policy. (Let's admit it, Republicans were a little parochial and weak on the mental department until the neocons brought their powerful intellects to their aid.)

The ideal Republican will be a firm and courageous moderate in all things. He will not have any ideas or principles other than making sure the rich keep making money. He will have some policies, made up by advertising agencies, infallibly "moderate," meaningless, and to be forgotten once the marketing job (excuse me, election) is over.

He will not be guilty of any documented felonies that have not been hushed up and he will never, never be guilty of "extremism." Once the media have exposed a Republican President as not quite the Boy Scout he is expected to be, it is all over. Look at poor Tricky Dick. As the Republican Presidential candidate he will never, never accuse his Democratic opponent of extremism or anything bad. That would be not being a good sport. It would be extremism.

The ideal Republican will recognize, of course, that sodomy is now "respectable," while anti-gay bigotry cannot be countenanced by any good American. Those Republican voters who have not been paying attention to the progress in recent years in what is respectable will just have to get to with the program and quit their belly-aching. Besides, Republican leaders have more gay relatives than the Democrats. But he must never let the Republican voters suspect that he is not one of them—is anything other than a brave defender of American family values.

So we have the man who will carry on the great tradition of Republican statesmanship—John Fremont, Horace Greeley, U.S. Grant, James G. Blaine, Chester Arthur, Warren Harding, Cal Coolidge, Alf Landon, Earl Warren, Gerald Ford, Bob Dole, Jack Kemp, the Bushes, John Boehner and Mitt Romney.

Let's not worry about any problem with the Democrats. It seems that Hillary Clinton is finally out of the running. It only took the American public a quarter of a century to figure out that she is Not a Very Nice Person. Of course, the minority has had the White House for eight years and might not want to give it up. There are an awful lot of power and perks there and opportunities galore to stick it to the majority. But surely they will play fair— it's the Republicans turn after all.

I can just see it now—the Republican convention of 2016—delegates standing on their chairs cheering "the next President of the United States"— Pence of Indiana.

HISTORY QUIZ—AMERICAN PRESIDENTS

What American President launched a massive invasion of another country that posed no threat, and without a declaration of war?

What President raised a huge army at his own will without the approval of Congress?

What President started a war of choice in violation of every principle of Christian just war teaching?

What President said that he had to violate the Constitution in order to save it?

What President declared the elected legislatures of thirteen States to be "combinations" of criminals that he had to suppress?

What President said he was indifferent to slavery but would use any force necessary to collect taxes?

What President sent combat troops from the battlefield to bombard and occupy New York City?

What President sent the Army to arrest in the middle of the night thousands of private citizens for expressing their opinions? And held them incommunicado in military prisons with total denial of due process of law? And had his soldiers destroy newspaper plants?

What President was the first ruler in the civilized world to make medicine a contraband of war?

What President signed for his cronies special licenses to purchase valuable cotton from an enemy country even though he had forbidden such trade and punished other people for the same practice?

What President refused medical care and food to his own soldiers held by the enemy country?

What President presided over the bombardment and house-by-house destruction of cities and towns that were undefended and not military targets?

What President's forces deliberately targeted women and children and destroyed their housing, food supply, and private belongings?

What President's occupying forces engaged in imprisonment, torture, and execution of civilians and seizing them as hostages?

Under what President did the Army have the largest number of criminals, mercenaries, and foreigners?

Who was the first American President to plot the assassination of an opposing head of state?

Who had the least affiliation with Christianity of any American President and blamed God for starting the war over which he presided?

What President voted for and praised a law which forbade black people from settling in his State?

What President said that all black people should be expelled from the United States because they could never be full-fledged citizens?

What President was the first to force citizens to accept as legal money pieces of paper unbacked by gold or silver?

Who was the first President to institute an income tax?

Who was the first President to pile up a national debt too vast to be paid off in a generation?

Who is considered almost universally as the greatest American President, indeed as the greatest American of all times and as a world hero of democracy?

What Republican predecessor is President Obama most often compared to?

This is a take-home quiz.

Please grade yourself.

THE PROBLEM OF THE LESSER EVIL

I F YOU HAD BET ME six months ago that the grassroots disaffection in the Republican party, as demonstrated by the "Tea Party" movement, would guarantee a responsive nominee for President, you would have lost. I am no prophet, just an observer with some historical perspective. I would have bet on Romney against all comers. The Republican party almost always returns to its roots (like a dog to its vomit) and selects a wealthy liberal from the Deep North to head the ticket.

The media and the "front-runners" colluded to ensure than no real political debate made it to the airwaves during the sideshow of the primaries, which had no purpose except to make us poor dupes in the boondocks think that we had some input. It will be the same in the national convention, which will not be a political event but a scripted advertisement.

Isn't it curious that the Republican party will have a presidential nominee from Massachusetts, which (along with its spawn, Connecticut and Rhode Island) has the smallest and most atypical Republican electorate of any State?

For a long time, the state capitalists and political hacks who controlled the Republican party dominated American politics by an appeal to respectability against the evil party of "Rum, Romanism, and Rebellion." The desire for respectable conformity being the predominant American characteristic, according to Tocqueville in the 19th century and Solzhenitsyn in the 20th.

In the 1960s George Wallace demonstrated the electoral strength of anti-liberal sentiment, which brought forth a new marketing strategy from the party leadership, a pretense to "conservatism." Ronald Reagan, leading a revolt from the Heartland, was forced to take a rich liberal from the Deep North as his running mate and successor. When it came George H.W. Bush's turn to lead the ticket, his vice-president was another rich boy from the Deep North, repackaged as a "conservative," which nobody had thought of him as before.

The party leaders are now presented with a problem. To what extent should they recognise the disaffected grassroots? Will they exclude them entirely from the campaign, relying on anti-Obama sentiment to bring in their votes for "the lesser evil," a strategy that has worked every time? Or give them some insincere lip-service to keep them quiet? We will be able to get some idea from the vice-presidential nominee. I would bet on some Quayle-like pseudo-conservative, probably another rich boy from the Deep North, who might happen to live elsewhere now.

There is a genuine moral case to make, that when the only choice is between two evils, to select the lesser one is a correct action. However, careful consideration is required in discerning which evil is the lesser, as well as recognition that the lesser evil is still an evil.

I hold no brief for Obama, who I do not even consider to be a proper American citizen.

However, I note that the incumbent seems actually to believe in the leftist nostrums he espouses, disguising them no more than normal in conventional politics. Every position that Romney will take in the coming campaign, especially in so close an election as is likely, will certainly be an insincere marketing strategy that holds us poor dupes from the boondocks in barely-hidden cynical contempt True, a President Romney will not appoint any Sotomaier to the Supreme Court, just a Souter or Blackmun, which for all practical purposes will be the same thing. I can think of only one significant difference between Obama and Romney, the purported "lesser evil." Obama is slightly less likely to start and illegal, unjust, and unnecessary war.

THE REDS AND THE BLUES

I T HAS BECOME COMMONPLACE to observe that the American people are now divided into two distinct camps, roughly approximated by the opposing voters in the recent presidential election. The Blues, concentrated in the northern tier and Pacific states, are the progressives, marching on into the brave new world of polymorphous hedonism and limitless ethnic transformation. We Reds are people who like the Old American way of life and think that Christian morality is still valid. The division and its likely progression are beautifully laid out by Mr. Patrick Buchanan in his latest book, *Suicide of a Superpower.*

Where a population is critically divided, one might hope for a bit of compromise and restraint, live and let live. We Red States, generally speaking, might be happy to leave the Blue States alone to do their own thing. But the Blues will never leave us alone. First, it is in their economic interest to continue to transfer as much as possible of the national product to their constituents. Second, they are sure that their way is the true and right way and that we Reds are merely ignorant yahoos who must be educated, and if necessary coerced, into the light.

France is divided into irreconcilable political ideologies, but it manages to get along because of its cultural core. Switzerland consists of three or four different ethnic groups, but unlike the United States, it has a genuine federalism, that allows mutual cooperation as needed. None of this is to be hoped for in the American situation. We the governed literally have no appeal against centralized executive and judicial authorities that fall just short of controlling the air that we breath. History seems to be stacked against us Reds. The last election may have registered the high point of our political power. The demographics, whether measured by age group or ethnicity, are all against us. Nearly all the institutions of our society are under effective control of the Blue

161

elite. The Culture War is over and we lost. Most of our troops surrendered without a fight.

There is still a greater obstacle to building political power to defend the Red States. That is the Republican party, an historical hold-over, an electioneering machine which collects the Red vote but does not represent it. Both parties are eager to sacrifice the people to the bankers. Both to varying degrees support the global empire, which they will never give up except in the wake of a major disaster, and probably not even then. Both are indifferent to the ongoing marginalization of the old American identity. Both participate in the pervasive distortion of public discourse known as Political Correctness. They have cooperated in erecting the surveillance/police state that has almost rendered individual liberty null and void on the pretense of making us secure.

The true solution to our present dilemma would be a dismantling of the federal monopoly of power—secession, nullification, devolution, what you will. This is, at least at the moment, a poor hope, though there are stirrings that could bear fruit. The Blues will not relinquish power and a great many among the Reds are people unable to tell the difference between "My country, right or wrong," and "the government, right or wrong." Or between national defense and foreign aggression.

I am much tempted to fall back on a couple of old Southern sayings: "There's not a dime's worth of difference" and "Frankly, Scarlett, I don't give a damn." Just color me gray. (2012)

AMERICA AS A PROPOSITION NATION: FACING OUR SUPERSTITIONS

THERE IS A POPULAR SUPERSTITION that defines America as a "Proposition Nation," created and proclaimed by the obiter dicta about "all men" in the second sentence of the 1776 Declaration that the 13 colonies "are and of right ought to be free and independent States."

Is America a Proposition Nation? No, for the very simple reason that there is no such thing in human life. Like the unicorn, it can be imagined, and some people may even claim to have seen it, but it cannot really exist.

But if we agree that America is not something thought up, we are still left with the problem of defining what exactly we mean when we say "America." Granted, America is a place, or rather a sort of a place or many sorts of places, inhabited by people of flesh and blood. But is it a country, a nation, a people in the substantive meaning of those terms? This seems to me the vital question of the moment. What if Americans are not a nation and the best unifying identity they can hope for is as a Proposition? What if a whole series of presidents have declared that they have seen flocks of lovely, graceful unicorns grazing on the White House lawn, and millions of people have believed them?

The history of the United States makes clear, it seems to me, that America, while not a Proposition Nation, has long been governed as a Proposition Regime. Lincoln defined America as a Proposition and defended his war of conquest as the means of preserving the government that was allegedly upholding that Proposition. He was not speaking for traditional American constitutionalism and republicanism or for the America that had been known up to that point.

He appealed most strongly to the revolutionary agendas of three particular groups among Americans: profiteers who stood to benefit from a protected market and a highly centralized capital-friendly government; New Englanders, who, from their very beginning as a self-proclaimed Shining City Upon a Hill, had endowed America with a unique and sacred missionary role in history, under their direction; and German immigrants and other national unification state worshipers, bastard offspring of the French Revolution, who had achieved a considerable ideological transformation of the North during the 1850s.

Together, they created the Proposition Regime—resting upon appealing inventions about an America of endless prosperity and progress, and uniquely virtuous violence in stamping out the grapes of wrath.

These types are still in power today. Clearly, the Proposition provided a cover for some interests at the expense of others. As Lincoln spoke, his party was fashioning a system by which the natural resources, enterprise, and labour of the country would be largely in the custody of Eastern financiers.

Devotees of the Proposition Regime always define it in terms of Lincoln's pretty words about equality and government of, by, and for the people. But its real spokesman is General Sherman, whose ruminations I highly recommend to anyone who really wants to understand how we got here. General Sherman made it clear that all who disobeyed the government of the Proposition Regime were rebels against the sacred who quite literally deserved nothing except extermination.

Moving forward a few decades from Lincoln and Sherman, we find that America is known as distinguishable by her characteristic philosophy—pragmatism. Americans, among all the peoples of the world, are especially noted as a nation of pragmatists. And what is pragmatism but a methodological Proposition—indifferent to the humane values that have traditionally bound societies together?

Move forward a few more decades, and we find Henry Ford. Could there possibly be a more archetypal American? Ford said in 1916 that "History is more or less bunk. It's tradition. We don't want tradition.

We want to live in the present, and the only history that is worth a tinker's damn is the history we make today." His statement was widely reported and much admired at the time.

Forward a few more years, and we have another archetypal American, Calvin Coolidge, who proclaimed that "The business of America is business." So that is what America is about—not blood or kin, not tradition or history, not honour, not liberty, not the Constitution, not a common culture, but a Proposition about getting and spending. A Southerner at the time pointed out the cultural impoverishment revealed in Coolidge's dull, materialist reaction on his visit to the Alamo. The novelist Owen Wister commented, "Eternal vigilance cannot watch liberty and the ticker [tape] at the same time."

Can we really deny that Lincoln, Sherman, Ford, Coolidge, and George W. Bush represent the prevailing and controlling substance of what we know as "America"? That they are the mainstream of American history and the central and revered American tradition? And yet, despite all the power of the Proposition Regime, those of us over about 60 years of age can remember another America that was quite real, or at least seemed to be. But if we are honest with ourselves, we must admit that what we remember as our country no longer exists. The America of the 1940s and 50s is as dead and gone as the America of the 1850s.

If Americans were a people, could they possibly be persuaded that wasting their blood and treasure in the invasion of a remote country that has done us no harm is somehow their duty and in their interest?

Millions of inhabitants of the invented America of global democratic benevolence apparently do believe this and are sending fellow citizens to die for their fantasy. Indeed, for more than a century, the idea of the Proposition Nation has provided a rationale for wars that were seldom wanted by, or in the interests of, the citizens. The Proposition was born in conquest and has from the beginning had a militantly missionary nature.

If Americans were a People, would almost two thirds of the Senate have voted, as they recently did, for so-called immigration reform that will literally displace our grandchildren with Third World coolie labour? The "nation of immigrants," another invented Proposition, has clearly trumped whatever may be left of our America. Once more, the pretty words serve particular interests against the will and well-being of the citizens. After all, the real business of America is business. The other day, I heard the President say that the amnesty of illegal immigrants must be passed because that is the kind of thing "America should do." Not my America. But my entire lifetime as a citizen has been nothing but a relentless series of defeats of my America by his America. It has rightly been observed that a vague thing labeled "values" has been substituted for traditional society as the thing conservatives are supposed to conserve. But this is not an invention of the Neocons. They could not plant their poisonous flowers with any hope of a successful crop unless the ground was ready.

What if their American Proposition is not an aberration but the true American tradition and the only viable theme for a society such as America has become in our lifetime? Is there, somewhere out there, a demographic, economic, social, political, cultural, uninvented America, real and potent enough to reassert herself and reclaim her right to exist and prevail? That seems to me a fundamental and pressing question. Maybe there is. I would like to believe that there is. But I am yet to be convinced. If there is not, we will have to agree with the Proposition as put forward by the colonel in *Full Metal Jacket*: "Inside every gook is an American wanting to get out."

A FEW MODEST SUGGESTIONS FOR THE TRUMP ADMINISTRATION

ORDER WITHDRAWAL OF TROOPS and materiel from Afghanistan and Iraq. (Without bringing the indigenous population with you.) Perhaps a small CIA presence might be maintained just for intelligence-gathering, which is what they are supposed to be doing anyway.

Join with Russia to destroy ISIS in preparation for a withdrawal from Syria. This will allow the indigenous forces to sort it out among themselves and also create a constructive relationship with Russia that will be of great future benefit for many reasons.

Accept that Islamic factions will always be at war with each other and the U.S. should not meddle except in a strictly defensive necessity. Our relations with the Mideast should be simply to buy oil, without political or military interference and without manipulation of policy by American "global" corporations.

Find measures to decrease the presence and influence of Saudia Arabia, the Gulf States, and Israel on domestic American politics. A law forbidding ex-members of Congress and executive officials from becoming lobbyists for foreign powers would be wholesome and democratic. Forbid foreigners, particularly Chinese, from holding positions in defense institutions and related companies.

Make plans to convert NATO to a European organization with only symbolic American presence; and stop expanding military assets onto Russia's borders. The Europeans would welcome the end of our interference and would be encouraged to once more look to their own defense. Needless agitation of Russia is literally insane and can only serve those in power, not America.

Build the wall.

Also beef up border control at airports, getting rid of silly unproductive procedures and restoring sensible profiling.

Take intensive measures to identify and deport ALL illegal immigrants and visa over-stayers, particularly such Muslims as perpetrated 9/11 and other atrocities. Along with a strict ban on Muslim immigrants. This can be done within present law. Actually enforce E-verify against employers.

Abolish HEW. Make an intensive review of all federal GRANT programs and pass laws to eliminate them. The federal government has created a large cohort of institutions that are dependent on taxpayer cash for completely non-essential, unconstitutional, and often destructive purposes. This would have the wholesome effect of making state legislatures work seriously on their governmental responsibilities, and also of returning charity and culture to private sponsorship. A line-item veto will be seen as essential for this goal.

Conduct a truly INDEPENDENT review of the Federal Reserve and alternative policies for managing the currency. Also, reinstate the Glass-Steagall Act separating commercial and investment banking; staff the Securities Exchange Commission with independent people; and demand that the bailed-out Banksters repay more of their loot from the Treasury.

Relieve all the top brass of the armed forces and search for commanders who are genuine soldiers and patriots and not a— kissing bureaucrats. (Especially the idiots who made soldiers wear high heels in "sensitivity training.") Immediately revoke all measures that place women in harm's way. This is the least something that can be done to restore honour to the U.S. military. Develop really effective special forces instead of over-reliance on technology.

Take steps to reduce the federal debt and particularly the burden of interest payments to people who contribute nothing, take no risk, and pay no taxes.

Pay off and eliminate foreign bond-holders. This may require scaling down of the debt.

It is well-known that Washington DC and its suburban counties are the wealthiest area of the U.S. The elimination of bureaucrats and scaling down of federal salaries and perks will be essential to getting control of the budget.

Take steps to eliminate the outdated policy of "affirmative action." In the meantime, make sure that it applies only to native-born African Americans.

Study ways to greatly increase the licensing of a multitude of new media so as to break the unhealthy and undemocratic domination of public discussion by a few networks.

Perhaps most important, craft legislation that removes most of the life of the people from the jurisdiction of the Supreme Court. Begin impeachment against the numerous federal judges who have shown contempt for the Constitution and a predilection toward tyrannical usurpations of power over the people.

These few modest suggestions should keep President Trump and his team busy for the first 100 days. Of course, nothing can be accomplished unless Trump finds and appoints new people, knowledgeable and dedicated, rather than the usual run of Republican hacks waiting in line for perks and power.

ABOUT THE AUTHOR

DR. CLYDE WILSON is Emeritus Distinguished Professor of History of the University of South Carolina, where he served from 1971 to 2006. He holds a Ph.D. from the University of North Carolina at Chapel Hill. He recently completed editing of a 28-volume edition of *The Papers of John C. Calhoun* which has received high praise for quality. He is author or editor of more than a dozen other books and over 600 articles, essays, and reviews in a variety of books and journals, and has lectured all over the U.S. and in Europe, many of his lectures having been recorded online and on CDs and DVDs.

Dr. Wilson directed 17 doctoral dissertations, a number of which have been published. Books written or edited include *Why the South Will Survive*, *Carolina Cavalier: The Life and Mind of James Johnston Pettigrew*, *The Essential Calhoun*, three volumes of *The Dictionary of Literary Biography* on American Historians, *From Union to Empire: Essays in the Jeffersonian Tradition*, *Defending Dixie: Essays in Southern History and Culture*, *Chronicles of the South* and *The Yankee Problem*.

Dr. Wilson is founding director of the Society of Independent Southern Historians; former president of the St. George Tucker Society for Southern Studies; recipient of the Bostick Prize for Contributions to South Carolina Letters, of the first annual John Randolph Society Lifetime Achievement Award, and of the Robert E. Lee Medal of the Sons of Confederate Veterans. He is M.E. Bradford Distinguished Professor of the Abbeville Institute; Contributing Editor of *Chronicles: A Magazine of American Culture;* founding dean of the Stephen D. Lee Institute, educational arm of the Sons of Confederate Veterans; and co-founder of Shotwell Publishing.

Dr. Wilson has two grown daughters, an excellent son-in-law, and two outstanding grandsons. He lives in the Dutch Fork of South Carolina, not far from the Santee Swamp where Francis Marion and his men rested between raids on the first invader.

AVAILABLE FROM SHOTWELL

Non-Fiction:

Nullification: Reclaiming Consent of the Governed by Clyde N. Wilson (The Wilson Files 2)

The Yankee Problem: An American Dilemma by Clyde N. Wilson (The Wilson Files 1)

Maryland, My Maryland: The Cultural Cleansing of a Small Southern State by Joyce Bennett

Washington's KKK: The Union League During Southern Reconstruction by John Chodes

When the Yankees Come: Former South Carolina Slaves Remember Sherman's Invasion. Edited with Introduction by Paul C. Graham

Southerner, Take Your Stand! by John Vinson

Lies My Teacher Told Me: The True History of the War for Southern Independence by Clyde N. Wilson

Emancipation Hell: The Tragedy Wrought By Lincoln's Emancipation Proclamation by Kirkpatrick Sale

Southern Independence. Why War? - The War to Prevent Southern Independence by Dr. Charles T. Pace

Fiction:

A New England Romance & Other Southern Studies by Randall Ivey (Green Altar Books)

PUBLISHER'S NOTE

IF YOU ENJOYED THIS BOOK or found it useful, interesting, or informative, we'd be very grateful if you would post a brief review of it on the retailer's website, Good Reads, Social Media, or anywhere else you think might help us get the word out.

In the current political and cultural climate, it is important that we get accurate, Southern friendly material into the hands of our friends and neighbours. *Your support can really make a difference* in helping us unapologetically celebrate and defend our Southern heritage, culture, history, and home!

———————

For more information, or to sign-up for notification of forthcoming titles, please visit us at

WWW.SHOTWELLPUBLISHING.COM

Thank You for Your Support!